PRACTICAL HEALING

FOR

MIND AND BODY.

A Complete Treatise on the Principles and Practice
of Healing by a Knowledge of
Divine Law.

By Jane W. Yarnall.

SEVENTH EDITION, REVISED.

I came that they might have life and that they might have it more abundantly.   ST. JOHN, X. 10.

CHICAGO.
JANE W. YARNALL, Publisher.
1902.

COPYRIGHT, 1891, BY J. W. YARNALL.

MANUFACTURED BY
W. B. CONKEY CO., CHICAGO.

INTRODUCTION.

EVERY student who takes up the study of the laws of mind, will find that many of his life-long views and ideas must give place to the truths we find in the new dispensation.

This will not be hard to do when you remember that no practical help or comfort has ever come to you from the old way of thinking and doing, and we know that great help and comfort do come from the new way. A willingness to give up the false way is in the highest degree essential to one who takes up the study with honest, sincere desire to grasp an understanding of its principles.

Prejudice gives a false coloring to all things, thus blinding us to their true character.

One who reads with prejudice against any theme will not get the right coloring, because the bias of such minds closes every avenue through which the truth might otherwise find entrance.

To read with honest candor and sincere desire for truth regardless of what the world may say or think, will open your mind to what otherwise would not appeal to your judgment at all.

It is universally admitted by all people of judgment and candor that former ways of thinking, believing and doing, have always been more or less disappointing, and have not brought the comfort and happiness the race has always hungered for.

The plans and aims men set out with are acknowledged to be more or less a failure.

Each year of a man's life is an experiment, and every new scheme has its doubtful side. Men go on in life beset with fear and uncertainty enough to weaken their efforts to a great extent, all because true principles are not understood and brought to bear upon their undertakings.

Each year brings an increase of restlessness and dissatisfaction, all of which reflects upon the physical. Nervous prostration has become almost as common as less serious maladies, and may be said to originate from the same cause, viz., Ignorance of truth,

The numerous forms of disease that show forth upon the human race are all due to man's transgression of the righteous law, or law of right; and man transgresses the righteous law because he has a false conception regarding that law.

He falsely believes he is doing what will best satisfy his desires and aspirations.

His false beliefs are the result of false education; and false impressions are often inherited from ancestors many generations back, according to mortality's ways.

The prophet declares "They taught their tongue to speak lies, and their children have inherited lies."

These false ways are now showing forth in the wretchedness and misery we see about us in the form of disease, discord, insanity and crime.

In no age of the world has there ever been so much insanity (so-called) as now. Each year there is a demand for enlarged accommodations for these victims of false education.

Such facts are cited only as proof that there is

somewhere a monstrous flaw in the ways and methods of men.

Some great mistake in the problem of life has set the whole machinery into confusion.

Harmony is the law of the universe, and it should be the business of every man, woman and child to seek a knowledge of that law.

"Man was created upright, but he sought out many inventions."

He was also created with dominion over all things, and his false and foolish inventions destroyed his consciousness of that dominion.

As long as man maintains a consciousness of his divine nature, he will think and act in line with that divine harmony which gives dominion; otherwise the mortal gains supremacy and he loses his dominion. In other words, when he allows the carnal mind to rule he is out of harmony with Divine Law.

"The carnal mind is enmity against God," not subject to Divine Law at all; and while the carnal mind rules, the life problem will be full of mistakes.

The carnal nature has held the reins over mankind for so many centuries that the children of earth have scarcely any conception of true principles in relation to life, and it remained for the few earnest, self-sacrificing seekers for truth of this 19th century to discover a way to solve this great problem of life.

It is the sole aim of this science of all sciences, to correct the false ways and mistakes of human judgment that have brought discord and confusion to the children of men, and when we prove by demonstration that a knowledge of these principles will bring harmony out of discord, and give health for sickness, and strength for weakness, by correcting the false ways, every one must admit that we have reached a step far in advance of any previous reasoning, and yet we have only begun to know the power of understanding truth.

To be able to secure and maintain a perfect state of health and harmony for mind and body, is the first step, and all have to take this first step before they are qualified for the higher ones; at the same time the principles by which you heal your body and regulate your temper are the same; and the earnest student will soon learn to control circumstances, and regulate all the affairs of life.

A careful study of the principles herein explained, will enable any honest, earnest student to heal all so-called diseased conditions of their own bodies, or those of their friends and neighbers, and also to remove ill tempers and correct all immoral tendencies.

By the knowledge and faithful practice of these principles, life may be made one continual blessing to yourself and every one about you, because the very nature of the law is harmony.

J. W. Y.

ADVICE TO READER.

INASMUCH as many who read these lessons will not have access to oral instruction, we feel called upon to advise them not only to *read the lessons*, but study every statement over and over till its meaning is perfectly clear.

The full meaning very seldom dawns upon the conscious mind with the first reading, and *often* not with the second or third; but with earnest concentration and perseverence, the light will shine upon every statement, and the principles will become so fixed in the mind that you will become one with them, and they will spring to your aid in every emergency.

The discipline given at the end of the third lesson is most essential to all students who want to make these principles practical in their lives, and the more thoroughly you familiarize your thoughts with the statements, and train your mind to reason in harmony with them at all times, the better results will follow your efforts in the study.

Repetition brings concentration; and when you have mastered every statement, and feel at one with the principles laid down, you will have no difficulty in healing, either yourself or others, and you will be able to demonstrate over all seeming difficulties, and finally you will live exempt from the need of healing, because you will know better than to be sick. J. W. Y.

NOTE.

THE principles embodied in these lessons, as taught by the author, have restored hundreds of miserable invalids to perfect health; many of whom have become efficient teachers and healers; and we feel assured that the careful study of them will do the same for thousands who still know not the way.

As a text book for teachers, as an instructor in healing, and as a healer of all physical maladies and mental inharmonies, I most respectfully offer this message to the world.

J. W. YARNALL.

LESSON I.

"Attend to my words; * * * for they are life unto those that find them and health to all their flesh."

TO gain a practical knowledge of the principles herein set forth, one has to be willing to begin at the very alphabet of truth, as beginning right is a matter of vital importance.

This philosophy of healing by understanding divine law, is based on man's sonship to God as *Mind, Spirit, First Cause*, which are all names of Deity.

Man is the offspring of Divine Mind, and the image and likeness of the same; therefore, we want to reason all the way in harmony with that statement.

To consider with deliberation what constitutes mind in the perfection we ascribe to Deity, we are forced to the conclusion that mind is the underlying substance from which emanates every attribute of Divinity, *Life, Truth, Love, Intelligence, Wisdom,* and *Purity;* all of which fill the universe and tend continually to good for the children of men.

As man in his essential nature is designed to be and to act perfectly as the image and likeness of God, all imperfect action and being are contrary to God's design; contrary to God's will. This philosophy is called by various names; among which are Metaphysical Science, Divine Science, Christian Science, Mental Science, Mind Cure, etc., all of which mean very much the same, and all of which claim to believe in and follow the Christ method of healing. The fundamental principles of this gospel of healing forbids any claim of personal distinction in the way of discovery or leadership, but teaches perfect freedom and equality, and like the Master urges the right of every one to find the Christ within for themselves regardless of name or school; and while we do not hold to the name "Christian Science" (because of the *assumed* exclusive right to that name by a certain class of Scientists) we still hold most firmly to the Christ Science as the "Science of Mind."

Jesus was called the Christ because he was the anointed One, who was to embody the Principle of Truth in the flesh, and teach true principles in such purity as had never been taught before, to a world so shadowed by ignorance as to have no conception of truth as a principle by which peace and harmony could be restored to mankind.

That portion of the civilized world that claim to be followers of Christ are, as a rule, proud and boastful of being Christians; that is, they seem to feel that they stand on a higher plane morally, intellectually and spiritually, than the people of other religions; and whether they live up to their highest or not, there is a feeling of confident assurance that the teachings of Christ are *true*, and that He was the master mind. All admit that He was the incomparable teacher of true principles.

He said, "I am the way, the truth and the life."

His early followers called him "*the master*," and he is still spoken of as the "Master."

We speak of the famous artists as the old masters, because of their superior talent in one especial branch of art.

The master musician is master of harmony in music only.

The master in painting is master of harmony in color and design only.

The master mechanic is master of machinery only; and so on through every branch of learning each one may be master of some one principle, but Jesus the Christ was master of all true principles, and understood and taught how to set principles to work harmoniously without material aids, and as all his teachings are absolutely true, we do well to call him THE MASTER.

As believers in his teaching it becomes us to look carefully into the way we are understanding his instruction, and see if we are walking consistently with it.

Every promise he made has certain conditions attached which must be met, and the condition which will bring us freedom is, knowledge of truth as he taught it. "Ye shall know the truth, and the truth shall make you free."

We are not to gauge our course of action, nor our beliefs by what we see other professing Christians do and think, but aim to know what is true for ourselves, and thus educate the judgment to see clearly how principles work in our lives.

He did not promise the freedom by depending upon what some one else knew or believed.

He meant of course that every one should understand and develop their own powers of mind, which powers are the gift of God to his children, to whom he gave dominion over all the earth.

The Psalmist said, "Thou gavest him dominion over all things, and hast put all things under his feet."

We have never been taught our birth-right in regard to this dominion until now, and it is in this Christian philosophy *only* that it is taught *now*.

Without a knowledge of this divine power we are in bondage to ignorance; *with* it we are made free, and we then have the mind that was in Christ, and can do the works He did.

"Let the same mind be in you that was in Christ Jesus our Lord," is the admonition of the Apostle Paul.

Jesus never taught nor acted from any human authority; He never quoted the sayings nor practiced the forms of the great Rabbis of his time; He never referred his hearers for example to the Scribes and Pharisees (who were in those days the acknowledged authority on all matters of religion), but warned his disciples against their teaching and practices.

He knew they perverted the teachings of Scripture, and did not recognize the necessity of serving truth, but made forms and ceremony of great importance, thus corrupting the minds of the people by leading them into false ways, encouraging hypocrisy and deceit, and ignoring righteousness and truth.

In the study of this system we find Truth to be the great working principle, without which there can be no harmony, and we find an understanding of its working qualities essential in using it, else the Saviour would never have made the knowledge of truth necessary to freedom, for instead of adhering to the forms and traditions of the Scribes and Pharisees he taught principles, and did away with the cold formality that was so lacking in Spirit.

How few of the teachers of Christian doctrines have set their reasoning faculties to work to find out how truth is going to make us free; therefore the Christian religion, as taught for centuries past, has lacked the practical quality that was intended for every nation, tongue, and people to know; and its clergymen have very largely gone back to the ceremonious ways so characteristic of the Scribes and Pharisees, besides bearing a close resemblance to them in the narrowness, bigotry, and intolerance they exhibit toward this practical Christianity. They do not and can never expect to carry the signs of *true believers* in Christ, while going so contrary to the principles he taught.

Jesus must have foreseen the faithless, half-hearted service that would prevail to such an extent when he asked with such prophetic pathos, "When the son of man cometh, shall he find faith in the earth?"

This lack of faith in what truth will do for us has always stood like an impenetrable cloud of darkness between the conscious mind of man, and the good things he desires.

We are not required to exercise a blind faith in what we cannot understand, but our faith is based upon philosophical reasoning.

To understand is to be able to give a reason for the hope within us.

This philosophy, from first to last, is pure reasoning based upon the premise that all the world admit is true, viz.: the omnipotence and omnipresence of God as Spirit, and man as the offspring, the likeness and image of God.

As God is Mind, and man is the image and likeness of God, man is also mind in his essential nature, and he possesses the attributes of God consciously, in proportion as he recognizes and acknowledges them and lives in harmony with Divine law.

Man was given dominion over all flesh in the beginning, and still retains it, providing he lives in accord with the principles of truth.

Harmony is the law of the universe. Harmony in the earth-life is Divine law manifest, and when true principles are understood and acted upon, perfect harmony of mind and body is the result.

To consider more definitely the nature and

character of God, we need to think of Him as the great center and source of all that is good for mankind, as the sun is the center and source of light and heat for the world.

The triune principle, Life, Truth and Love, constitutes all that is essential as the great source of good, from whence flows or radiates all goodness and perfection, filling all space with the good we desire; and as no such thing as evil, or falsity, or disease, or pain, or discord, can possibly proceed from Life, Truth and Love, when all space is filled with it, we begin to wonder where such things come from, as they *seem*.

There seems to be a conflict between what the senses tell us and what reason says. Which shall we believe? How shall we decide?

A great Jewish teacher and philosopher, who was considered very wise, once said: "When thy senses tell thee what thy reason denies, reject the testimony of thy senses and trust only to thy reason."

Again, this accords with the admonition of Jesus. He said: "Judge not according to appearance, but judge righteous judgement," which means according to righteous reasoning.

The wise sayings of all generations agree.

Solomon said: "Man was made upright, but he sought out many inventions," and one of the inventions of man is this mortal, human, carnal mind, that leads us away from true principles, and causes us to judge by appearance as we are commanded *not* to do.

Paul seemed to understand this carnal nature, and by him we learn that the carnal mind is always at enmity against God, and is not subject to the law of God; neither, indeed, can be. Why? Because it is not a creation of God's, and is *not* a reality.

God never created anything that was at enmity against another of his creations, because that would be contrary to the law of harmony, which is the law of love, the law of God, the *only* law in the universe.

When we trust this carnal mind we are led away from truth, and are continually led to believe in the false as real, and the more falsity we harbor in the conscious mind, the more liable we are to show forth the falsity in our physical conditions, because the physical is merely the outward expression of what we think and believe.

Solomon very wisely said of man: "As he thinketh in his heart, so is he."

If man thinks falsely and believes what is false, his thoughts and beliefs must be mirrored in his life, either in bodily conditions or his environments, and the only remedy for such conditions is in knowing the true way.

The human family have been for so many ages under the dominion of error that it amounts to bondage.

Ignorance of truth is bondage to error always.

It has been very wisely and truly said that "Ignorance of truth is the cause of all misery."

This was the inspired utterance of Gautama Buddha, five hundred years before Jesus said, "Ye shall know the truth, and the truth shall make you free."

The wise and inspired of all ages agree most wonderfully in their sayings, which proves that all truth is *one*, and no statements of absolute truth can possibly conflict, no matter who makes them, where they are made, nor in what age of the world.

Now if knowing truth will make us free, surely it is wise to seek the knowledge, for all desire freedom.

As all our miseries are the result of not knowing truth, we need to know in what way erroneous thinking and believing affects us physically and otherwise.

Every reasoning mind will admit the fact that the emotions of the conscious mind act with instant effect upon the functions of the body through the circulation. For instance, *Fear*, when produced by a sudden shock, will stop the action of the heart *instantly*, for the moment.

The function of the heart (as you know) is to carry on a continual pumping process, which must be *unceasing* to be in harmony with physical law.

If the fear is of a forboding character, and is accompanied with dread and apprehension, it acts differently, and involves other functions as well as the heart.

If the fear amounts to a great terror of some approaching and inevitable danger, the effect is still different.

Terror dries up certain secretions, and has been known to completely destroy the secretion of coloring matter for the hair in a few hours, leaving it perfectly white, and we cannot reasonably suppose that such terror would act on that one function alone, but would affect the whole system more or less, as is the case with fear of every shade.

Anger is also very destructive to harmony of body as well as mind. Violent anger is known to suspend the digestion completely for the time, by closing up the avenues through which the gastric juice flows into the stomach, thereby causing the pent up fluid to become more or less poisonous,

We often hear people say: "My blood fairly boiled with anger." They speak more truly than they know, for there is a boiling, seething condition of the fluids that changes the character of the blood *at once*, turning it to acid poison, which often shows forth in humors and blotches and boils, and unsightly swellings. And then the patient wonders why he is so grievously afflicted, and will generally resort to some blood purifier (so called), while all he needs is to live serenely and control his passions.

Every ungodly emotion of the mind produces an effect that is more or less destructive to health and harmony, always acting through the functions which are dependent upon the states of the conscious mind for their harmonious action.

It seems needless to mention the numerous ways in which the functions of the body are disturbed by the emotions and passions; and we leave the reader to consider in his own way, and perhaps by his own experience, how selfishness, greed, envy, jealousy, hatred, malice, lust and deceit destroy the peace and tranquillity of mind, and thus affect the functional departments of the whole system.

Many who see this and know it is true, are not aware that every organ, every bone, muscle and nerve, and every joint and movement of the body, are wholly dependent for sustenance and support upon the harmonious action of those functions, while (as stated above) the functions are wholly dependent upon the states of the conscious mind. Then of course mind is the responsible agent, and your reason tells you the need of correcting the errors of the mind, and training it to control its passions and emotions.

We have been taught by physiologists in the past that the brain secretes the mind as the liver secretes bile, which is a foolish and ridiculous statement that requires very little reasoning to prove its fallacy.

The brain is the instrument of the mind, with which it directs every act of the body, consciously, the same as the eye is the instrument of the mind with which we see consciously, and the ear to hear consciously.

The mind uses the brain to think upon what it sees with the eye, and hears with the ear.

Mind is that which is real and eternal. Mind is of God, and cannot perish.

If mind was dependent upon the brain for its origin, it could bear no resemblance to the Divine Mind.

The brain is of the earth earthy, and is nourished and sustained in the same manner as other physical organs, and is affected more or less as they are by the passions and emotions of the mind, while mind is not a thing of earth at all, nor is it dependent upon earth for its sustenance and renewal.

Mind is not dependent upon matter. Mind is Spirit, and is renewed in the image and after the likeness of Infinite Mind, if so be that we reject the false carnal nature and allow truth to rule.

"To be carnally minded is death."

The carnal mind is mortal, but when corrected of its carnal false nature it is renewed in the likeness of God, and when *fully* corrected of *all* mortal error, we have the mind that was in Christ Jesus, and it is no longer carnal, or mortal.

The process of regeneration is the passing from ignorance to knowledge; or from death unto life.

We put off the old man with his deeds, and put on the new man, renewed in the likeness and image of God.

The mortal puts on immortality by training the mind to consciously know realities, and the change is mirrored upon the body.

The peace and tranquillity that come with a full realization of true principles, begin to act upon the functions at once, and very soon the whole physical body rejoices in perfect peace and harmony, which is all accomplished by the renewing of the mind from the source of all mind.

The blessings and benefits of understanding these principles are threefold:

Healing all our infirmities.
Correcting all immoralities.
Brightening our intellectual faculties.

And the result is peace of mind, knowledge of truth and health of body.

As you proceed in the study of this Divine law, you will see how unmistakably dependent the body is for health upon this peace of mind and knowledge of truth.

It is very common for people to take up the study solely for the healing, and they often say *at first*, that they care nothing at all for the moral or religious aspect of the subject, but they want to get well, or they want to heal their family and friends. They say: "I can get all the moral and religious training I want in my church and in society."

They don't know that their physical disorders are all due to the foolishness, ignorance and false ideas they have always been surrounded with in society, as well as in their religious associations.

They don't know that purified morals and spiritual awakening to what is real and true regarding themselves, their origin, and their powers, accomplish the desired change in bodily conditions, more quickly and *more* perfectly when they take up the study for the grand truth there is in it, than for the health it brings.

The greater our love for The Principle, the greater the benefit.

Many have such lofty pride of intellect that they feel humiliated to find themselves ignorant of such grand truths, when they have spent years of time and mints of money in the famous institutions of learning and among the learned men of the world in the acquirement of knowledge, but it makes no difference how much pride of learning, nor how lofty and conceited one is, all have to go back to first principles, and begin at the bottom round of the ladder. You will find all that is true in your great education will be useful to you, and you will have the judgment to detect the false and the firmness to reject it if you are true to the principles of science

Some three hundred years ago one of the great and learned men of France, Des Cartes, became aware that much of the great learning he had spent years to acquire was false and of no use to him; so he set himself to work in great earnestness to find a way to obliterate from his mind all that was false in his fine education. He spent much time in solitude, communing with the great unseen Intelligence, asking for guidance, and in the silence there came to him a message in words so plain he could not misunderstand; it was to the effect that *all future discoveries of true law wait upon the knowledge of the Occult laws of healing.* This was a true revelation.

No matter how wise, how intellectual, or how selfsatisfied we may be, we will find that true wisdom is only found through this law of healing as Jesus taught it; and this knowledge is the first step every one must take.

Those who think to shirk this first step because of some foolish pride or lofty conceit, will never reach the peace of mind that is so essential to health.

"Except ye become as little children ye shall in no wise enter into" this knowledge, which is the kingdom of heaven.

You want to assume and declare at the outset in this study, that mind controls all.

Mind builds the body true or false according as we think truly or falsely of God, of His attributes, and of our relation to Him, and our dependence upon Him as the only Life, the only Intelligence, the only Power in the universe.

As all things are dependent upon the Life Principle, it is the problem of life we are dealing with continually, and especially in this study are we aiming to solve the life problem.

We have never known or *heard* of any one who has solved it with full and entire satisfaction.

Every one goes through this mortal experience with more or less regret that he had not known better how his plans and aims would result.

No matter how carefully his plans were considered, nor how systematic his methods, there would always be more or less disappointment in the outcome.

Something would always go wrong and bring worry and vexation, and often failure, in spite of systematic plans and what seemed wise counsel.

In many cases the confusion has brought dissensions and quarrels, and animosities of the most grievous character; often insanity and suicide.

We see such conditions multiplied daily and yearly, all because this life problem has been wrought on a false basis; because people do not understand the principles of the problem they labor so hard to solve; they work in the dark.

In every case, "ignorance of truth" will be found "the cause of all the misery."

No matter how much confidence one has in his own human judgment, he is constantly reminded of its limitation; and torture his brain as he will in his efforts to plan a wise course of action, he finds himself limited both in judgment and in powers to execute; and the doubts and fears regarding the outcome begin to crowd upon him, and often take possession, and soon the physical begins to succumb; then the fear of sickness augments the trouble, and he begins to realize how helpless he is in his human wisdom, while death stares him in the face as the culmination of his ignorance.

Fear of sickness and fear of death have always been the great "Bugbear" of the human race.

People are always making their plans with the if. "If I *live* and keep my health."

Even the most prosperous carry this burden of fear and anxiety.

Fear of reverses, fear of being defrauded, fear of accident, fear of sickness, and worse than all, fear of death, and fear of eternal punishment after death.

How can we make people know there is nothing but ignorance to fear?

If people will only seek an understanding of the principle of life, health, peace and prosperity, so as to proceed with confidence in all their undertakings, the burden of fear and apprehension will be removed.

The study of the life principle is the study of First Cause, the study of God, which means the study of all Good, and nothing but the absolute Good; the eternal verities of life.

All the old prophets and mighty men of Israel, Moses, Elijah, Joshua, David, Daniel, and others, obtained their powers through the study of *First Cause*, *Divine Law*, or *God*. No matter what we call It, if we only understand It, and acknowledge It as the only power, It is the only study worth while.

We begin at the very outset with the strange bold statement that only the good is real and true; and no matter how the world may dispute the statement, no matter how many wise sayings they may quote to prove our statement false, no matter how many events they may hold up as evidence that we are in error, no matter how much they scorn and ridicule the statement, and even hint at lunacy, we shall *stand* by the statement and finally prove it to them.

This statement is the basis for much severe criticism from the "*so called*" Orthodox churches or clergymen, notwithstanding the fact that they set out exactly according to Science in the statement of the omnipotence and omnipresence of God.

We find it reasonable and logical to stand by the statement we set out with, while *they* consider it orthodox to turn and deny it. They don't seem to realize that their statement means exactly the same as when we say, "Only the good is real and true."

God means, The Good; Omnipotence means, *all power;* and Omnipresence means, *everywhere present;* therefore the good is the only Power, the only Presence. God is all in all. There is none beside Him.

When will the Christian world reason according to what they claim to believe?

They *must* see the truth some time; and when they do honestly accept it, and fearlessly and openly declare it, their eyes will be opened to see the glaring contradictions which now characterize their teachings, and all those old fears will have given place to confidence, courage, and love.

In all ages of the world since our Bible has been known, the truly wise and spiritually minded have seen and known that back of all the physical transactions and material descriptions in the scriptures, there is a deep spiritual significance that does not appear on the surface to the careless reader at all. And, strange as it may seem, the orthodox clergymen of the 19th century who met in London a few years ago to agree upon a new revision of the scriptures, actually agreed that there was a spiritual meaning back of those scriptural statements that had always been so difficult to explain; but we never hear of any of them going any deeper into the mystery than the simple admission of its symbolism, while much of the richness and beauty of the scriptures is lost by not understanding the language of symbolism.

The Persians, the Hindoos, Egyptians, Chinese, and all sacred writings are said to give the story of the creation virtually the same as it is in our Genesis.

"In the beginning God created."

The world have always supposed that there was an actual beginning; that a time of beginning was meant, while the matter of time was not considered at all.

God knows no such thing as time. He is from everlasting to everlasting; and to think of time in connection with God and His creation is to set up a limit which belongs alone to human conception. Time is an invention of the human intellect only.

When man has cast off the carnal nature and become consciously one with Divine Principle, then will come to pass the prophecy in Rev. "There shall be no more time," which means that man will lose his *mis*conception and see things aright.

The story in Genesis has been reduced to the understanding of all by translating the language to read thus:

"In the great forever, without beginning of years or end of days, God is creating, or The Good creates."

The whole statement in its true sense comes from an understanding of God as Spirit—as First Cause—the Absolute Principle of Good; and all responsibility in creation rests upon the Infinite God.

The word God, or the name of Deity, in any language means The *Good*. The word God with one "o" embraces the *all of good*, while good with two "o's" may only embrace one or more of the God-like attributes.

Notice, the *Good* is the Creative Principle. All nations and people who believe in God at all, believe Him to be good, and wise, and powerful, and yet much of the religious instruction we have heard regarding God tends to the impression that He is cruel, vindictive, vengeful, and very weak and variable about some things. The teachings have not always harmonized with the statement of Divine Being, which they set out with.

I repeat, that every *true* statement will agree with every *other* true statement.

The fact that any statements ever conflict, is the evidence that one or the other is in error.

If we declare that God is omnipotent goodness and love, and afterward admit a belief in another power that is *not* good, we virtually deny the first statement.

God would not be God if there could be another power.

Omnipotence, Omniscience, and Omnipresence are the Essentials of Deity, and without them there could be no God. These are names belonging to God alone, and must not be given to another.

"Thou shalt have no other Gods before me."

We are commanded to "Acknowledge God in all our ways," which we cannot do while we admit an evil power or presence.

When we hear the minister in his Sunday morning prayer at church thank God that he is permitted to come into His holy presence on this occasion, as we often hear them, we notice at once that he has virtually denied the presence of God during the week.

Of course, such admissions are unintentional, but it betrays his misconception of God.

The personal God of *his* conception could not be omnipresent; therefore, he could not be God. No one can conceive of a personal God being omnipresent.

The prophet Isaiah said, "Come now and let us reason together." Let us do the same.

We say God is Spirit; all agree that God is

Spirit, and the eyes of flesh cannot see Spirit; but the eyes of flesh *can* see person.

God is Life, Truth, and Love, all of which are Spirit, or Principle, unseen to the eyes of flesh, but not unknown to spiritual perception.

God is the great center and source of all that is good, and nothing but good flows or radiates from that center.

Even His name is The Good.

This Trinity of Unity, Life, Truth, and Love, sends forth rays of purity and goodness in power, wisdom, health, strength, harmony, and peace, and fills all space with the Divine essence which makes the omnipresent Good.

By reasoning in this way we see how impossible it would be for the essence of all purity and goodness to produce impurity, or evil, or foolishness, or sickness, or weakness, or pain, or discord; therefore it is not a true supposition.

God is the only Substance in the universe, and all Principle is one with the substance from which it proceeds.

Substance is good because it is God. Life is God, and Life is omnipresent good; even the smallest imaginable space is filled with Life as Principle.

Truth is God, and Truth is omnipresent good. Love is God, and Love is omnipresent good.

All the old philosophers and bards say God is Truth, and God is Love, and no one dares to say that Love as Divine Principle is not good, for Love is God.

Intelligence is also good and God is Intelligence. Wisdom is good and God is Wisdom.

Notice—All these divine names are of a character that is eternal, and imperishable.

No power in the universe can destroy the Principle of Life, Truth, Love, Wisdom or Intelligence; they are absolutely imperishable, because they are God.

What is this Substance we call God that underlies all that *is?* It is Mind; "Mind is good, and the good is God always, thus you see God is also Mind, and Mind is the great First Cause, the omnipresent creative Principle, the only Substance in the universe, the only Intelligence, the only Power, the only Deity, the Good."

Remember all these attributes of perfection mentioned as the different qualities of Mind, the Wisdom, Power, Intelligence, etc., belong to God alone; therefore we have no right to attribute Wisdom, Power, Intelligence, etc., to any other being; and when you mention any power opposed to the good, you violate the command, "Thou shalt have no other Gods before me." You are giving power and omnipresence to something that has no place nor existence, except in the delusions of mortal mind, which is the mind that is carnal and false, and not at all subject to the law of the Good.

How can there be another Power when God is omnipotent?

Every time the statement is made that there is an evil power, there is a flat contradiction of God's omnipotence.

This is the point at which we have to part company with the ideas of orthodoxy, which ideas have held the whole Christian world in bondage for 1800 years. We have been guilty of idolatry without knowing it. That is, we have believed in a Power other than the God we profess to believe in as the only Power.

We have not been consistent. We have been working at this great problem of life on a false basis, and then we wonder and complain at the confusion and misery.

We have taken the evidence of the senses while ignorant of true law, which is judging by appearance, instead of righteous reasoning.

We have been so long under the dominion of error that the false way of thinking seems true, and the true way seems foolish and absurd till we reason it out and prove it true.

No one has ever proved his dominion over

material conditions by mortality's ways, and never will.

The flesh man is not the image and likeness of God, to whom He gave dominion.

The flesh man can have no such dominion. That which is the image and likeness of God is mind, and mind is the dominant man who is to control and subdue all that is beneath him, and surely the flesh man is nothing without the mind that controls and dominates it. We have never been taught our birth-right in this respect until *now*, and it is in this Philosophy or Science alone, that we are taught how we may be masters of every situation, and that we have complete dominion over our environments if we claim it as our inheritance and understand the law by which we may use the divine gift.

Through the powers of mind when trained to harmonize with divine law, we build our world around us as we will.

We live eternally in the now; we need no preparation for a world to come if we think and live truly *now*. It is always *now* and always *will be*.

The Master never taught us to concern ourselves about to-morrow, or about any future life, but spoke always of the now.

He said, "*Now* is the day of salvation;" which means, if you accept the truths I teach, you are saved *now*.

FOR MIND AND BODY. 41

What are you saved from by accepting the truth? From all the discords that mortal error produces; from sickness, pain, misfortune, crime and poverty; all of which are conditions that lead deathward, while, "the gift of God is eternal life" *now*.

Perfect health, peace and prosperity, all depend upon our recognition and acknowledgement of it through understanding divine law, which is truth. The Master said, "Whosoever *will*, may come and drink of the water of life freely."

What is it to drink of the water of life?

It is to take into the mind *consciously* the understanding and realization that we are heirs of Eternal Life, and that we have the right to claim it now.

We drink of the water of life whenever we take into the mind a truth that satisfies our thirst for righteousness.

We drink of the water of life when we accept the gospel of good news in the spirit he gave it.

To "drink of the water of life" is a figure of speech, and it is the spirit of the words that gives the life, not the letter.

And now, dear reader, if you have not already reasoned out your problem, begin at once. Go to yourself and in the silence realize what God is, and what your relation to Him is, and never admit the reality of any seeming obstacle to your understanding.

In this way you will find the divinity within you. In this way you will find yourself *in Spirit* the child of God, and like Job, when all else has failed you, you will say, "I would talk with God; I would reason with the Almighty;" and like Job you will find restored health, peace and prosperity beyond your most sanguine expectations. This reasoning with the Almighty that brings peace is the discipline we advise for every student of truth.

It is wise to set apart a portion of each day, from a quarter of an hour to an hour or more, if convenient, alone in the silence, and concentrate the mind upon this reasoning with the Almighty.

In doing so you call forth the best there is within you; you find the Divine self of you.

Then you begin to consciously realize that all that is God-created is good; All that is God-created is imperishable, indestructible and eternal.

All that is God-created is perfect and without blemish.

Meditate upon this with full confidence that it is true, and do not try to call up the proofs that seem to contradict it.

In the next lesson you will find a reasoning that will prove these statements true, and with faithful self discipline, you will soon prove them to your own consciousness.

CURED BY THESE LESSONS.

Something over three years ago a Baptist clergyman, aged 65 years, who had been a victim of consumption (so called) for many years, at times very low and again able to preach occasionally, was finally reduced to a condition considered absolutely hopeless by his family and by physicians. He became interested in this true science, and consulted Dr. Yarnall regarding his chances for a longer lease on life than what the doctors and his family considered possible. He said he was not at all afraid to die, but he felt that it was very unbecoming in one who professed godliness to carry such a miserable body. The principles of the science were briefly explained, and all the help we could give was tendered him. He had a few treatments, and then entered a class, attending every lesson promptly. Before the close of the course of twelve lessons he declared himself perfectly healed.

His testimony before the class at the close of the lessons was to the effect that although he had been a preacher of the gospel of Christ (as he had formerly understood it) for many years, he, like the majority of Christians, had virtually denied the practical part of the gospel by living contrary to what he preached. As he expressed it: "After preaching or hearing a good sermon we all go home and act all the week as if we did not believe a word of it."

A large cavity in his lung, from which he was expectorating most freely and offensively, was perfectly healed in a few days, and in five weeks from the time he entered the class he was installed as pastor of a new church, and is still preaching and in good health. When asked if he should preach these principles, he answered that he should preach Christ as he *now* understood Christianity from the teaching he had listened to in this class, and if people did not like his preaching the whole gospel as he now understood it, they would have to listen to some one else. He has since then taught many classes, and being a highly educated theologian, his Bible lessons, taught in the light of the new Science, have been very uplifting and enlightening.

LESSON II.

"Ye shall know the truth, and the truth shall make you free."

KNOWLEDGE OF TRUTH IS FREEDOM.

IN the previous lesson the statement is made that ignorance of truth is bondage to error. All bondage is mortal error, or mortal belief in limitation, because of the false education, false believing, and false ideas regarding the nature and character of the God we worship.

No matter how sincerely devout we may be in the worship of our God, if we have false ideas, or a wrong conception of God, we are worshiping a false God, and all our appeals are as vain as if made to a god of wood or stone; our condition is then one of bondage, because of the error. We are thus demonstrably ignorant of the *true* God.

A false idea concerning God is the first or fundamental error of the race, because all other falsities grow out of it.

If we believe God to be a cruel, vindictive despot, ready to slay or punish us on the slightest pretext, we cannot love Him, for such belief makes us fear Him instead. "Perfect love casts out fear."

If we believe that He allows an adversary to destroy His children and His works, and bring confusion and misery upon them, we accuse Him of weakness, or deny His omnipotence, and this also brings fear. We cannot have full confidence in His power for good if we believe in an opposing power.

If we believe we are under the watchful eye of an accusing God, we cannot be at peace, because we are continually afraid of offending Him. Fear is the great destroyer of peace, and all are in bondage to fear who harbor false ideas of God.

Peace of mind is one of the first essentials to perfect health of body, because the body is built perfectly or imperfectly, according to the truth or falsity harbored in the conscious mind; in other words, the body is the outward expression of the thoughts and beliefs of the mind.

Every kind of false belief engenders fear. Every error in our problem of life hides the truth from our consciousness, and we are lost in doubt, apprehension and fear, which is a state exactly opposite to one of peace, all of which is bondage; and under this bondage we grow irritable; we believe in limitation instead of freedom; we imagine injuries, we become suspicious, we grow envious and jealous of some one who seems to enjoy what *we* seem to lack, and we make ourselves miserable, sick and depressed over it.

When sickness overtakes us and we are prostrated with fever, the doctor will call it a bilious attack or malarial fever, and we accept his diagnosis as the true solution, because we have never been taught that envy and jealousy and suspicion in the mind open the door to such poisons as malaria and contagion.

No one has ever taught us that an irritable temper and petulant, disagreeable ways would produce acids in the blood, liable to show forth in rheumatism or gout.

We were never taught that deceitfulness and hypocrisy would show forth in various ways upon the body or in the family; often upon the most innocent and lovely character in the family.

No one ever taught us that anger, hatred, and malice long indulged were liable to culminate in cancers, tumors, or ulcers that physicians consider incurable; nor that dread and apprehension *long endured* were liable to result in paralysis; and that melancholy and brooding over trouble destroy vitality and cause nervous debility, and sometimes insanity; all of which are only an appearance, therefore false.

Why do such passions and emotions produce such effects in appearance?

Simply because the conscious mind of man entertains erroneous opinions regarding the "powers that be."

If we did not believe in a power that could injure us, or wrong us in some way, we should not be irritable, suspicious, envious or jealous.

If we did not fear that our rights would be interfered with, we should not get angry, nor indulge in hatred and malice.

In short, if we did not believe in the power of evil, we should not be afraid; we are never afraid of the good.

The effect of fear upon the functions of the body (whether conscious or unconscious), is the greatest predisposing cause of disease, although it may be wholly reflected from other minds, as is the case with infants and imbeciles.

And what are the evils so generally feared? All evil is supposed to be of the devil; then comes the question, Who or what is the devil?

Jesus said the devil was the father of lies.

A lie has no reality and can do no harm, only as we believe in it, and all that proceeds from the devil is as the lie himself, false; therefore, what we fear as evil is only a myth, and needs only a firm rejection of its claims to destroy its influence and obliterate its effects.

Sickness, pain, and all discords are the result of believing in the reality of evil, and are only appearances, false as the devil is false; who is the father of all such conditions.

The word Father implies parentage, and the offspring is supposed to bear a likeness to the parent.

The father of all evil being in every sense false, all the resultant conditions are also false.

"An evil tree cannot produce good fruit."

But you say, "The evil is a reality all the same." No, not so.

Let us reason together again.

We have already stated that only the good is real and true, and we aim to make no statements that will not bear the light of reason. We desire to measure every statement by the one infallible rule already mentioned, viz., Truth is God, and God is Good, and the Good is all that is real and true, and whatever does not harmonize, or have its Origin in the triune Principle, Life, Truth and Love, (which is God, and from which flows and radiates all goodness and wisdom) is *not* true, is *not* real, and must be rejected as false.

Now, according to this line of reasoning it is only the carnal mortal nature that sees or recognizes evil at all; and we read that the carnal mind is enmity against God, not subject to the law of God; and according to Scripture it is "as prone to err as the sparks to fly upward." It is not to be depended upon at all. The carnal nature is pure selfishness, and selfishness may be said to be the devil, as it is directly or indirectly the parent of all wrong doing.

It is selfishness that prompts one to be dishonest. It is selfishness that prompts one to lie. It is selfishness that prompts one to slander and traduce his neighbor. It is selfishness that makes a man a tyrant. It is selfishness that makes one vain, envious and jealous. It is selfishness that makes one suspicious and censorious.

The selfish person is never happy, and never radiates happiness to others, because the selfish propensity is carnal and false, and must produce its likeness in false conditions.

The grasping, selfish nature, that aims to make everything bend to his desire for gain regardless of the rights of his neighbor, is blind to the fact that he will some day have to pay the penalty of his greed in some way that will more than balance his accounts. He may have secured the material wealth, and he may for a time revel in fancied enjoyment of it, but the day of reckoning will come, unless he turns and wipes out the wrongs by which he gained his selfish ends.

When sickness, misfortune and death overtake him and take away his dearest treasure, he never dreams that in the past, in his dishonest, selfish greed, he set an inexorable law to work, which by his own ignorance and folly was aimed at what he held most dear.

He falsely believed he was gaining satisfaction by gaining wealth regardless of the right.

"As ye sow, so also shall ye reap."

Another phase of selfish blindness to truth is represented by the man who is always in a state of worry and anxiety, in anticipation of loss, of misfortune, of accident; always on the verge of some calamity which will surely come if he is faithful with his fears. He sets the law to work by a similar process, and like Job the very thing he feared comes to pass. He may be honest and upright in his dealings, and pious and Godly as he understands Godliness, but the same false ideas have held him in bondage to fear, and he will finally succumb to nervous prostration. Then the doctor will dose him with morphine to stupefy his senses, because he does not know what ails him. He never dreams that confidence in God, and a realization of his own divine rights, would restore the nerves to their normal state.

The feeling of grief and depression because of some fancied wrong, or because your feelings are hurt, is purely selfish, and frequently culminates in sick headaches and finally in spinal troubles if continued persistently.

The business man whose cares and perplexities have robbed him of his rest and worried him into a state of distraction and despair and final prostration, generally goes to his physician for advice, and although the doctor admits that the great mental strain has been the predisposing cause of his prostration, he will dose him with the most nauseating drugs, as if that would set his mind at rest. He will put the medicine in the stomach that is to act upon the mind to restore courge and tranquillity and judgment.

According to physics this is a very wise proceeding. According to metaphysics it is a very foolish one.

He might just as well give a man a dose of Castor Oil to cure him of stealing, because in either case the cause of the trouble is not reached at all.

A man steals because of a morbid belief that he wants something that is not his own; the belief is false, and when his mind is cured of that error he no longer desires what is not his own because he has learned that satisfaction never comes by wronging others.

The man who sinks under discouragement because of failure in his business schemes, believes in limitation and inability on his own account, which is another false belief, and the longer he entertains that belief the more he will weaken his efforts, and the deeper will he sink in discouragement. He has been trusting wholly to his human judgment and carnal desires, which are so prone to err. He does not understand true principles, nor consult the Christ within himself.

Christ is Truth, and *"Other foundation can no man lay."* Every scheme to be successful must be laid upon a true foundation; it must rest upon a true basis; and the failures of business schemes are all due to ignorance of truth.

We are now coming upon the time prophesied, that, "Judgment shall be laid to the line, and righteousness to the plummet."

The selfish greed for gain often blinds the man of business to the justice due his neighbor, and he is often heedless of the little stings of guilt that prick him, he is so intent upon the gain to himself, and all the time he thinks he is gathering riches to himself.

He doesn't know that every moment of his life the functions of his body are growing more and more discordant. He doesn't know that the delicate machinery of his anatomy is affected by every twinge of guilt, and by every unrighteous desire to acquire gain to the disadvantage of his neighbor.

He doesn't know that his fear lest some one gets the advantage of him in his business transactions, is setting his whole nervous system into discord; and when he is overwhelmed with confusion he still doesn't know that he is a slave to fear because of ignorance.

Ignorance of truth is what causes the mother to cover her unborn babe with fears of every imaginable evil condition, which so often leaves its impress in some frightful deformity. And often the children who are born with the most perfect physique, are followed through childhood and youth with fear and anxiety enough to crush out all vitality. No matter how well meant anxiety is, it is none the less crushing in its weight.

The whole world seems borne down with this weight of fear; fear of sickness, fear of accident, fear of misfortune, fear of poverty, fear of death, and, worse than all else, fear of eternal punishment after death by an angry God.

People of every grade and rank feel that death

stands ever ready to close in upon them and cut off the last hope.

Although people have always believed in the reality of these hard conditions, there have always been *some* who felt sure there ought to be a way out of them, but the way has never seemed clear till found in this wonderful law of mind, and in this we find that knowledge of truth does in reality make us free. Was ever so much meaning embraced in twelve simple words as when Jesus said, "Ye shall know the truth, and the truth shall make you free?"

It was his mission to the world to teach the truth that would make men free.

When brought before Pilate by the ignorant, angry mob to give an account of himself he said, "To this end was I born, and for this cause came I into the world, that I should bear witness to the truth."

He not only bore witness to the truth, but he demonstrated what truth would do for us by understanding it.

I have already stated that truth is a working principle that waits in the silence to be recognized. That is, it waits for the word or thought that will set it into action; just as the harp strings wait for the touch of the musician before they will give forth the harmony of sound.

Our part is to know truth; to understand the nature of that which works, and how to set it into action.

With this knowledge we find we may be liberated from all the undesirable conditions that result from ignorance of truth. We accomplish our salvation from all evil, from all fear of evil, and all danger from evil influences, by knowing truth and understanding its working power.

To many this may seem a very strange statement. It is only strange because it seems new, and there are only two ways of looking at it. It is either true or it is false. If it is true, those who understand can prove it true; if false, no one can prove it true, and we should be left to struggle on as before, and grope our way through ignorance and doubt without knowing the way out of bondage.

It is utterly out of the question for the human mind to be without beliefs of some kind, and the great and wise king Solomon said of man, "As he thinketh in his heart, so is he." Every man is going to think in line with his beliefs, and if he believes falsely he will think false thoughts; therefore, he will show forth false conditions. His body will express the character of his thoughts. Thought is the builder, and it builds true or false according to the beliefs and thoughts of the conscious mind. If he is ignorant of truth, he is liable to build falsely because he trusts to mortal sense.

Ignorance is not knowing, and the promise is that *knowing* truth will make us free.

How are we to *know* with certainty that we understand the truth in this matter?

By proving it.

Take the following statement of Being and study it over, analyze it, turn it over and over in your mind, and try and see every side, and every phase of it; try and realize what it all means, then make up your mind regarding it; whether you really and truly believe it or not. You will find that it agrees in every particular with the commonly accepted statements of the Christian denominations called orthodox.

THERE IS BUT ONE GOD, ONE LIFE, ONE TRUTH, ONE LOVE, ONE SUBSTANCE, AND ONE POWER, divinely Good, Omnipotent, Omniscient, and Omnipresent. Now, let us reason from this statement as a basis with full confidence that it is true.

If we say God is Omnipotent, and *mean* what we say, we deny the existence of any other power, because Omnipotence means all the power there is in existence.

When we say, God is Omniscience, we mean

that He *knows* all there is to know. When we say He is Omnipresent, it is the same as saying there is no other presence but the good, the true, the powerful, reliable, and substantial; and in this presence is intelligence, wisdom, peace, and purity.

To proceed in this line of reasoning we say we are the children of this great Life Principle we call God. We are the offspring, the branch of this omnipotent Mind, and all that we *have*, and all that we *are*, has its source in this universal Father; we can have *nothing* without Him; at the same time knowing that He has nothing to give but goodness.

To reason on the plane of mortal sense, the human intellect begins to ask, Whence comes the misery in its various forms, the sickness, the pain, the sorrow, the misfortune, poverty, crime, and the thousand and one difficulties that follow? Can all these things be said to come of thinking and believing falsely? Yes, every one of them.

You will notice that heretofore we have been taught that there was a great and wonderful evil power in personal form, stalking abroad unchecked through all the earth, and we have been made afraid of it by hearing so much about it; never losing our fear of it long enough to reason ourselves out of its grasp. We never knew we were denying the Omnipotence of God every time we admitted the power and presence of a Satan. We have never been taught to know just what is meant by the devil, and Satan, and the evil one so often referred to in the Scriptures by the various names given to the evil propensities of the carnal mind.

When we have made the statement of Being with an understanding of its import, we have virtually denied the reality of any evil power, and we ought to see that those evil conditions that *seem* so real only exist in imagination, and are the fruits of carnal error, or the outshowing of false ideas.

The object and aim of this Divine Science is to correct the mistaken beliefs of the conscious mind, which we call "mortal," and make it conscious of immortal truth; and in doing so we must examine into these seeming evils, and see how much claim they have to reality.

People in all ages of the world have had more or less of sickness, sorrow, misfortune and death, as such things are understood by mortal mind; and in all ages of the world people have sought to remedy such conditions without knowing the causes, therefore their seeking was in blindness and doubt.

They have always recognized sickness, pain

and sorrow as something to be feared and dreaded; as something *real*, something that must be met by resistance.

People utterly ignore the admonition of Jesus to "Resist not evil." In resisting it we acknowledge it as something, and that is all it asks.

The moment we recognize evil as something to fear, we give it a seeming power in mind, and thus we acknowledge another power other than the good we have stated as the only power. Power belongs to God alone; and "Thou shalt have no other Gods before me."

"Resist the devil, and he will flee from you." The devil is the evil propensity or evil impulse that prompts you to think and act falsely, thereby producing some false picture or some manifestation of your error in sickness, pain, or discord, which you are *not* to resist or recognize as a reality, inasmuch as it is only an appearance; the fruit of your error in *not* resisting the evil impulse named devil.

That evil propensity or evil impulse is the selfishness that must be conquered by denial. The Saviour made selfishness the most important denial. He said, "If any man would come after me (Truth), let him deny *himself*;" put self out of the question *utterly*.

The spirit of the word is what gives it life, and

it is because we have never understood the spirit of it that we find so little of the life-giving quality in the teachings of Jesus. Paul said very truly that the letter killeth, while the spirit giveth life. The life-giving quality is never lacking, but it is only found by those who catch the spirit of the teaching.

Even His words are spirit, and they are life; and to hold persistently to His words will awaken a realization of their true meaning. He said, "*If* a man KEEP my sayings." To KEEP His words and sayings in the mind, to hold to them, brings the reward in spiritual perception of truth.

Professing Christians in general are no more exempt from sickness and afflictions than those who have no belief in Christ at all, simply because they have never understood the meaning of His lessons, and have never earnestly KEPT His sayings, which has been more the result of not knowing, than of willful disobedience.

All suffering, misery, or discord betrays an ignorance of truth, while knowledge of truth saves us from the misery; makes us free.

In the search of mankind for better ways, all are seeking for truth without knowing it. Only truth will satisfy; only truth can make us free, and only by knowing truth can we set it into action.

The standard by which we are to judge as to what is true may be found in the Statement of Being, and whatever does not accord in every particular with that statement is not true, and must be rejected as false. Every circumstance, condition, or statement that comes up should be measured by this sure test and treated accordingly. If it is good and true, it will be found to agree with the divine Principle, from which all goodness and truth proceed.

No evil condition or circumstance can possibly proceed from Infinite Goodness, Truth and Love, therefore all evil conditions and circumstances are an outgrowth of false ways of thinking, and are only appearances that may be dissipated by the word of truth. As an illustration, this life problem may be likened to the simple problem in mathematics. If you believe ever so honestly that two and two are five, and you work your problem ever so carefully with that error running through it, your answer will be all wrong, of course. Then what is the remedy? You will erase the false answer; *rub it out* completely, and forget it; then if you are willing to be taught that two and two are four instead of five, and work your problem accordingly, the true answer will stand out as proof that you understand the true calculation.

Now, if we are willing to be taught the falseness of our old beliefs in evil (which show forth in disease and discord), and accept the true way to solve the life problem, we shall rub out all the discordant pictures made by the false ways, and establish health and harmony by the firm, true word.

The old false ideas and beliefs are the promptings of the carnal mind, and are therefore carnal in their effects. It is written, "To be carnally minded is death." To allow the demands of the flesh the mastery, is carnal. The sensuous pleasures of life are carnal. All sordid desires are carnal, because the end sought for is selfish and ungodly. Such are the ways that lead to death, as they are not in accord with true principles, and have not the spirit of life.

"To be spiritually-minded is life and peace." The spiritually-minded *look to Principle, understand* Principle, and trust the law that is set into action by knowing true Principle.

The conscious mind needs to be faithfully trained to distinguish between the divine in man and the visible fleshly shadow, the body; and to know that the divine child of God is "spiritual, *not material;*" that it is the spiritual man that is the image and likeness of God, and all of him that is *real* and *immortal*.

It is the carnal nature that supposes its body is the man, and we must convince the conscious mind that its body is only the unreal shadow of the human intellect. It is that changeable, perishable bundle of atoms which even in a state of perfect health and harmony only symbolizes the real man, and in its outward showing reveals the kind of thoughts and beliefs he harbors, according to the statement already made, that conscious mind is the builder of all bodily conditions, but the body is not the man. Man is Mind—Spirit, free, wise, immortal.

One of the greatest ethical teachers of the age has said very truly that all visible phenomena are but signs or symbols of things that are real, and that what we see is not the real thing at all; and he only is a philosopher to whom these things are distinct and true.

What *appears* is only to carnal sense, and to think of the physical body as the real self, is to be carnally minded, which is death.

Every one who holds to the physical as the man, expects to die; he makes all his plans with the expectation that *some* time death will overtake him and conquer.

There is *great dread* and *no peace* in anticipation of death to the materially minded; but "to be spiritually-minded is life and peace." It is simply a full realization of what is true and deathless as Spirit, and a willingness to let go of the material as the real; to reject its claims to reality because it lacks the qualities that are imperishable.

We become spiritually minded by denying all that is false, and harboring none but true thoughts.

The Apostle Paul admonished his disciples to "deny all ungodliness." which admonition is as much for us as for the early Christians; and whatever is opposed to spiritual perfection *is* ungodly. So we deny it. It is not true. Whatever is true is Godly, for God is Truth.

We must reason out this problem from the basic statements that all that *is*, is Spirit, and spirit is God, and God is all powerful and good, etc.

This realization is perceiving the things of the Spirit consciously; and this perception of spiritual perfection makes the physical body respond to the thought, and show forth the perfection we desire in health and harmony.

The child of God is spiritual, and no one can reasonably think of a child of God being sick, or lame, or miserable, and you must know that just in proportion as you realize the nothingness of the physical and the all-ness and perfection of Spirit, will you manifest perfection and health of body, for the body is the outshowing, the picturing forth of thought, whether true or false. Righteous thoughts and ideas produce symmetry and beauty as well as health.

In all the past ways and methods of seeking relief from disease and discord, we find that it has been sought in every way imaginable, except in obtaining an understanding of the principles and laws of life.

As the problem of life is the question we are dealing with, we need to understand the Life Principle; hence the need of simplifying what has been heretofore made so mysterious.

We think of that which pertains to our spiritual nature as something uncanny and mysterious, and are too prone to entertain a superstitious awe of the unseen forces that seem to work in such mystery, which need not be.

Dominion over all the earth is the God-given right of every child He created, without respect of persons, and we never lose our dominion except by departure from true Principle, or from divine law.

To know that we may understand the working of these unseen forces we call Divine Law, requires no more credulity (even on the plane of the human intellect), than to believe in the necessity of oxygen in the common air we breathe;

one is as invisible and intangible to the sight and touch as the other.

We are willing to belive in the vitalizing quality of oxygen, and that it is necessary to our physical welfare without any evidence except that *some one else* has discovered it; then let us by the consent of the intellect seek to know the still higher law which leads up to spiritual perception, and which demonstration proves to be righteous and true.

We also prove that ignorance of this law makes itself manifest in many ways besides in disease and pain.

Now if all our miseries are to be laid at the doors of ignorance, the first step in wisdom is to dispel the ignorance.

Ignorance is simply a state of mortal mind which disappears as soon as knowledge of truth is obtained.

Knowledge of truth is also a state of the conscious mind; and as ignorance shows forth in misery, and knowledge of truth shows forth in harmony, it is very clear that all good as well as all that seems evil depends upon right or wrong states of mind.

We have been taught in the past that the body controlled the mind more or less, while in science we learn that the mind has absolute control whether we are conscious of it or not.

In the new way we find life, health and peace, while the old false way has always tended to death.

We are constantly warned to prepare for death, and the fear of death *without* this doleful preparation is continually held over us to terrorize us into accepting some cruel dogma regarding the future life.

Even the most devout who claim implicit faith in the teachings of Christ see nothing in them except the great preparation for death; while in reality he taught the way to eternal life *here* and *now*, and said, "If a man keep my sayings, he shall never see death."

The right interpretation of the Scriptures leads the way to life, and the false way tends to death. Is it not time we should have a more rational faith?

It seems reasonable that Jesus should use material objects by which to illustrate the deeper spiritual meanings underlying his lessons, because of the simple minded character of His disciples, who knew nothing of spiritual things. So he taught them by comparing the things they *did* know and understand, to the unseen, spiritual realities.

He seemed never at a loss for some object in nature to use as a symbol of the spiritual truth he desired to illustrate.

We also find most of the teachings of the old prophets to be in Symbols which were seen in visions, and the beautiful lessons underlying those symbols are very significant to the spiritually minded.

The story of the creation in Genesis is also a study in symbolism. The earth itself and all its changes and movements, as recorded in the history of the creation, symbolize the conscious mind of man.

"The earth was without form and void, and darkness was upon the face of the deep; and the spirit of God moved upon the face of the waters, and God said Let there be light."

The word was all that was needed; the Law was perfect and good, and the word was necessary to set it into action. "The word was God."

Every true statement *we* make is the word of God.

Every command we make *in harmony with Divine law* is a command of God. It is God speaking through us. Jesus said, "My words are spirit, and they are life." We make *our* words spirit and life by letting the same mind be in us that was in Christ.

The words of Christ are words of truth, and truth is Divine Principle. Truth is God.

In this story of the creation the earth is the

symbol of the settled convictions of the human mind, while the waters symbolize the changing, conscious thoughts of the mind, and the darkness symbolizes a state of ignorance, doubt and uncertainty.

The spirit and the word mean the same, and it may be spoken to the better understanding of all by saying, "The word of Goodness moved upon the surface of the conscious mind of man (which was in a state of ignorance), and He said, Let there be knowledge, let the mind be enlightened.

Light is the symbol of knowledge. We *see*. We understand. We comprehend. We have the light of reason when the word of truth moves upon the conscious mind.

The darkness that brooded over the mind of man was ignorance. Simply a state of not knowing, a negative condition of mind that rendered him unconscious of the positive *knowledge* of good, of which light is the symbol.

When we *know* we are not in ignorance, but when ignorant of what is real and true, we are always believing in what is false, and the false beliefs are what we are now about to dispose of.

In order to make these lessons practical we shall be as explicit as possible in our manner of explaining what contradicts all our previous ways of thinking. Never mind the contradictions; we have always been in error, and it is wisdom to turn to truth. Only be sure and not contradict the truth by even an admission of error.

There are many false beliefs that have to be met and demolished before the mind is consciously set free.

We classify them into five principal errors, from which all other errors may be said to spring.

First, the whole human family have always believed in more than one power; in more than one governing force; in more than one lawgiver in the universe. Even after the repeated declaration that God is omnipotent and omnipresent, they turn and declare that there is an evil power that is in every way opposed to the good—to God.

Some even believe it to be a greater power than the good, and they do not seem to know that they have contradicted their first statement at all. Herein lies the *first* inconsistency of our old belief.

In science we prove this belief in an evil power to be false. It has its origin in the father of lies. A lie is simply a statement, appearance or influence that is devoid of truth.

It can have no power to deceive or mislead, except what is given it by believing it.

The human mind is prone to believe in the false, because it allows the carnal sense to judge by appearance.

As long as the conscious mind believes the false statement of an evil power, *appearances* will *seem* to corroborate and prove it, but that does not make it true; and as soon as the mind rejects the lie, and boldly repudiates its claim to power, it has no prop at all, and down it goes; it had no support at first except in mortal belief, which is, as before stated, *never reliable*.

Our business as children of truth is to remove that prop from every false belief by a bold denial of the reality of evil.

We slay the falsehood by denying it.

The only way that has ever been found effectual in obliterating a falsehood and its effects, is to give it the name it goes by and fearlessly hurl the truth at it till it dies; it has no right to even *seem* real.

One word of truth has more power than a thousand falsities, because the omnipotent God is in the truth, and the falsity has nothing but mortal belief to sustain it.

This false statement or belief regarding an evil power is the first falsehood we assail.

Take the statement of Being as a basis for argument, and with that *fully realized* all error will sink into oblivion.

Every student of truth should consider it a religious duty to set apart sufficient time each day for this discipline, and alone in the silence, declare over and over, and over again, "There is no power in evil; there is no reality in evil; *there is no evil.*" Choose any form of wording that seems best to you, only be sure to utterly destroy the belief in any evil power, and the reality of evil in any shape.

By persistent and earnest denial of evil in every form you will find yourself free from any fear of evil.

It is the character of truth (as a working principle) to make us free, by knowing and declaring it.

Repeat your denials earnestly and vehemently till you realize freedom.

We have never had any conception of the power of thought till we learn this wonderful law.

Knowing as we do that to believe in an evil power is to deny God's Omnipotence, therefore contrary to any logical reasoning, and knowing the power of thought, we find it consistent as followers of truth (Christ) to send out strong vehement thoughts as messengers of truth, to correct the error so universally believed in. Let our protest go out broadcast over the world and deny the falsehood.

Truth is an eternal principle. Truth is God, and the very nature of a true thought is deathless. It is a word of God. "My words shall not pass away.'

"Every thought sent out in the silence is charged with the character of the mind that sends it," and it goes forth to slay or make alive. If charged with that which is evil and false, its seeming influence is toward death, because of its carnal character. If charged with truth it is the deathless messenger that brings comfort and life, and blesses wherever it strikes. Who can fail to see their duty in this respect? Let every one who loves the truth proclaim it, by sending out the true thought strongly charged with the firm denial of any evil power, and repeat it over and over and over again.

Say it to your friends. Say it to your foes. Say it to your household. Say it to your neighbors. Say it to the community. Say it to the world at large. Say it daily, and hourly, and wherever the thought strikes that denies the reality and power of evil, declaring that the only power in the universe is good, the evil, the crime, and the sordid selfishness begins to die and fade away; characters begin to change; trouble and sorrow in the home, and injustice and oppressions fall away, hope steals in, and things begin to brighten, better days begin to dawn, simply because you have sent the Divine word of truth to erase the false, while you yourself will be doubly blessed by the sweet echo that comes back to you in the assurance that you have blessed others.

It is the majesty of the Principle you understand and proclaim that works the happy change from sorrow to joy, or from sickness to health, or from poverty to plenty. You set it into action by your true word spoken *or thought* in confidence.

It seems a strange law to many, but it is only strange because so new to our finite understanding. The law is Divine and has always been, but it has taken the race over 1800 years to fathom the mystery of its working.

The next error we attack is the belief that there is more than one substance in the universe.

All over the world the people who believe in God at all believe Him to be the only God, the only Life, the only Substance, *the All*. And yet right in the face of this statement they do virtually admit another substance.

If substance is that which underlies all that *is*, there can be no substance in matter. *God is the only Substance and God is Spirit.*

To be logical in our reasoning we cannot even

give the name Substance, nor the character of power and omnipresence to any other but God.

Substance, Power and Omnipresence belong to God alone. So the claim for matter as a reality is a false claim, and it stands for rejection.

We have been accustomed to think of material things as having substance, and to the sense of touch they seem very substantial, while in reality they are perishable and subject to continual change and decay, therefore they are as nothing to Spirit; for Spirit abideth forever. Spirit is the only Substance. Spirit is the great First Cause of all that is; the underlying substance which is God.

Declare with firmness that there is but one Substance in the universe, and that matter has no claim to reality.

When we think of the material body as something that can suffer pain, take cold, or be sick, we are giving it dominion over the mind, which is the false way that brings the discord. The body is not Substance, and it has no life or intelligence of itself; it cannot report pain except through the mortal mind which is a falsifyer; and if we allow the body to rule through mortal mind we are carnal and must die; but to declare the truth, will bring life and peace.

Deny this falsehood regarding the claims for

the body, by saying, "There is no reality in matter."

Repeat it over and over till you realize the utter nothingness of matter, and it will seem to dissolve and set you free from the weight, *actually* free, and then you begin to *know* that matter has no more dominion over you. It had none before in reality; only you thought you must consult it, as to what it should eat, and what it should drink, and about the cold, and the heat, and the dampness, and the malaria.

Learn to know that your body is not *you* at all. It is something that belongs to you; a possession of yours, something by which you express what you are.

You are mind, and *you* have dominion over all flesh, and you must know that your body is plastic to your word, or your way of thinking and believing, and you may build it as you will.

If your joints were swollen and warped and stiff and lame from Rheumatism, and you found you could reduce the swelling, and ease the pain, and make them flexible, and symmetrical and comfortable in every way just by denying the false claims of matter, and by speaking the true into showing, you begin to believe that *sure enough* matter is not a reality, and you refuse to allow it to rule any more.

You find that you have the mastery by thinking truly, and you begin to realize in how many ways you may use the true word to dissolve the error and destroy its effects.

When Paul and Silas were imprisoned for teaching this same truth, the prison doors were thrown open in response to their understanding of the laws of Spirit.

Bolts and bars were as nothing to them, because they knew there was no substance in matter.

This is the same law, and the errors regarding all material law must be dissolved before we can be free from the bondage of matter.

Flesh is but the expression of mind. If the mind be carnal the body will express the carnal ideas in disease, or discord. The spiritually minded express life, health, and peace in bodily conditions.

The third false belief of the race that stands for denial is, that the appearance we call matter has life, and intelligence. It has neither; and the case needs no argument. Deny it vigorously. Declare there is no life or intelligence in matter, for matter itself is only a seeming.

All who follow this discipline earnestly and understandingly begin to find that material things seem changed to them;' they begin to realize how fleeting and unreal matter is. How delusive all that pertains to matter is; to-day it seems so real, to-morrow it is gone like a dream.

Whatever has a true claim to life can never die, because life is eternal. Whatever has the elements of decay is not substance, and whatever fails is not intelligence, because pure intelligence is God, unchangeable and unfailing.

So we need not hesitate to say, "There is no life, substance, or intelligence in matter; all is mind."

The fourth false belief that must be denied is, that the unreal material body can see, hear, feel, taste and smell.

These senses are attributes of the conscious mind, which uses the body as the instrument of seeing, hearing, tasting, etc.

The conscious mind is *mortal* or *carnal* in proportion as it dwells in error, or lives to the flesh. It puts off the mortal and puts on immortality when it rises to the understanding that, "The flesh profiteth nothing;" and it has no claim to reality itself, until it is born into this realization of truth.

While in the carnal state it assumes responsibility and presumes to be mind, and reports pain, and thinks the pain is in the body, while in reality there is no pain, and mortal mind reports a lie, which lie accords with its false character.

Deny the pain, every time mortal mind makes such report, and you will soon prove it false.

The reason for such denial is, "*There is no sensation in matter.*" If you deny it firmly and boldly, the pain, the weariness, or whatever will vanish, and every time you conquer the false claim you are stronger for the next occasion.

Send out the mental protest to all the world, denying that matter has any sense of pain, and your word will reach some poor suffering body, who will wonder what has eased his pain so mysteriously.

You may never know it, but that makes no difference.

We now come to the fifth false belief of the human race.

It is the belief of the people all over the known world that we live in a world that was created by Divine Wisdom and Infinite Goodness; and that our world is governed by Divine Wisdom and Infinite Goodness; and that all space is filled with Divine Wisdom and Infinite Goodness, which is all true; but right in the face of this true statement there is a general belief in *sin, sickness* and *death*, and no one seems to notice that one statement contradicts the other.

It has been very wisely said that "we **miscreate** our own evils," and "All that we **are, is the result of what we have thought.**"

If sin, sickness and death are realities, in this world, then the former statement regarding Divine Wisdom and Infinite Goodness is not true.

It is mortal mind again that talks of sin, sickness and death. It is mortal mind that has invented *all* the false beliefs, and it is mortal mind that "*miscreates*" in every case; and no matter how *real* the evils may seem, it is only a "miscreation" of mortal mind, and it stands for rejection because it is false.

Deny it boldly. No matter what form it takes; *deny* it. And the more *real* it seems, the more persistent should be the denial. We are to judge *not according to appearance*, but judge righteously, which means according to righteous reasoning.

Let all your reasoning be from the one basis given in the statement of Being, and you will reason righteously.

The principal evils we have to deny are sin, sickness and death, because all minor evils have their origin in Sin first (which is error), then comes sickness, then death, all according to mortal belief, hence all false.

Declare in the silence over and over, "There is no sin. There is no sickness. There is no death"

There is no evil at all, for all that is not of God is false.

When you are tempted to doubt the righteousness of this practice of denials, just remember Paul's admonition to "Deny all ungodliness," and take his counsel in this as much as in any other matter.

Fear not to say "There is no evil; there is no sin; there is no pain; there is no sorrow; there is no poverty; there is no sickness; there is no death,"

We know these words are true, because we bring true and good conditions to pass by using them understandingly.

Some wicked cruel design is checked by timely denial of the evil impulse. Some mean, selfish act of injustice is made to die in shame and confusion. Some lustful impulse is smothered before it has time to be acted on, and some poor troubled heart is made glad and happy, and they wonder what has relieved them and made them so joyful and free; and to every one who faithfully uses the true word for the relief of humanity, comes the sweet assurance that every day brings added blessings home to them.

This practice of denials is only the first step. It is simply the beginning of discipline.

We have to tear down the false and remove the rubbish of false beliefs, before we can build truly upon the rock which is truth (Christ), and this is the discipline that every student of truth must practice before the mind is cleansed of error.

We must erase every picture of error from the body, by this treatment of the mind, before the harmonions conditions will show forth.

Begin at once, and mentally deny the reality of everything that conflicts in any way with omnipresent goodness, purity and love.

Give yourself this discipline *daily*, two or three times, if possible. It will bring you peace. It will make you free. It will open your heart to love. It will reveal to you powers you never dreamed of, and teach you how you may gain the mastery over all evil conditions and undesirable circumstances.

Never look upon this practice as foolish or irrational, but consider it as much the prayer to be delivered from evil as if worded after the old fashion of supplication. It is your desire to be delivered from evil that prompts the practice; and desire is prayer.

Your prayers in the old way have never been answered by restored health, because you still believed in, and feared the evil as a reality; you still believed in the reality of sickness and pain. You still believed in the reports of mortal mind.

But now you can say to the mortal carnal

nature in the language of Edwin Arnold's "Light of Asia,"

"But now, thou builder of this tabernacle,
Now I know thee who thou art;
Never shalt thou build again these walls of pain,
Nor lay fresh rafters on the clay;
Broken thy house is, and the ridge pole split,
Delusion fashioned it,
Safe pass I thence, deliverance to obtain."

PARALYSIS HEALED.

Four years ago a lady who had been for many years an invalid, partially paralyzed, using crutches when able to move at all, living constantly under the fear of sudden death from enlargement of the heart, which pressed the ribs and other bones out of their normal position, causing considerable deformity, and pronounced hopelessly incurable by many physicians, came into a class, and was perfectly healed in six days by simply listening to these lessons. Her crutches were laid aside immediately, and in a few days she was able to walk miles in calling upon her friends to tell them of her restoration and of the healing she had found in this new Science.

She began to heal at once with remarkable success, and is now an efficient teacher of the science.

LESSON III.

"Without the word was not anything made that was made."

WE have already considered the importance of using words that are true, or words that harmonize with divine law, and also the evil effects of using words that are not true.

When we speak of words in this connection we mean the import of your thoughts and ideas, as much as the word spoken audibly.

Paul's caution to Timothy to "hold fast to the form of sound words" could be heeded by us with the same profit,

There is great power in sound, true words, especially in *holding* them in the mind. Jesus said, "If ye abide in me, and *my words* abide in *you*, ye shall ask what ye will, and it shall be done unto you." To abide is to hold fast; to keep. Christ's words are all sound words; true words. Any true word is the word of God; of Christ; and the true word creates or makes manifest what we desire, while the false word or false idea "*miscreates*" that which makes us miserable.

Whatever is not true of Spirit is not true at all, although it may be a fact to mortal sense.

The power of thought has never been generally known; and until very recently it has not been considered a study of importance. We have never been taught until now that our opinions and beliefs regarding the peculiarities and shortcomings of our friends and neighbors tended to depress and discourage and even augment the disagreeable traits we so deplore, especially when speaking or thinking of them with condemnation and censure.

The criticisms so freely indulged, and the unkind and often malicious charges made against a neighbor or acquaintance, reflect upon them with most demoralizing effect, but more so upon ourselves. The very fact that you hold them in mind as mean, or selfish, or proud, or mercenary, or deceitful, tends to make them more so, and makes you more so also. Such mortal errors and disagreeable traits are never cured by recognition of them. " He that stoppeth his ears and shutteth his eyes from seeing evil, he shall dwell on high."

When we do see them and think of them as a reality we may be sure that there is something

FOR MIND AND BODY. 87

in our own nature that in some way recognizes its own, and although there may be an outward disapproval and even an abhorrence of the fault, there is a hidden fellowship with it, or we could not see it.

If we are pure in heart we shall see only the good.

Every accusing thought is a seed planted for evil fruiting, and with a knowledge of this law we *must* see our duty clearly. Cease to think evil at all. Cease to criticise or condemn any-one. Mentally deny what seems wrong, and only recognize or speak of that which is good, for only the good is true. To speak of the false or evil at all as a thing of reality is to give it the fellow-ship that is only due to truth and goodness.

To be always on the watch for something to criticise or condemn, not only destroys the moral integrity of the one so criticized, but it strikes back upon ourselves with redoubled effect.

When your dearest treasure, your precious and only child, is stricken with some terrible malady (so-called), diphtheria, perhaps, and you are stricken with terror of the probable fatal result, you moan and cry and bewail the cruel fate of your child, and wonder why God allows such innocence to suffer and die; never dreaming that this is the outshowing or reflex expression of your unkind and unjust condemnation of your friend or neighbor. You recognize the mortal error in your neighbor as a reality, and perhaps even magnify it on the mortal plane, and this is your reward.

"Only with thine eyes shalt thou behold and see the reward of the wicked."

That is, only the eyes of flesh can see the evil, while spiritual perception tells you it is not a reality. Spiritual perception enables you to know all evil as only a mirage or unreal picture of your error; and your error often falls most heavily on that which you hold most dear, and thus you suffer a self-inflicted punishment for your unrighteous thought, and then charge it to God.

Truly, "the way of the transgressor is hard," but thanks to the good Father, there is a way out of this bondage; a way open and free to all who will seek it.

In seeking it we simply open our eyes to the good and true, and close them against the evil and false. We utterly deny the reality of all evil or anything that can produce evil in appearance.

We never mind what unbelievers say about proving the reality of evil; never mind what they say about the reality of matter and the evidence of the senses,

They are reasoning according to appearance, and the true thinker reasons from spiritual perception.

He that is spiritual judgeth all things, yet he himself is judged of no man. So don't be weak and faithless; launch out boldly, and let reason instead of sensation be your guide.

Righteous reasoning is the shining forth of divine intelligence.

If you are weak and wavering and hesitate because of the hostility of your church, or your friends in the church, let reason guide you out of that weakness also.

Take comfort in the fact that they agree with all the first propositions of Science, and that you are sufficiently consistent to stand by those propositions and square every argument by them; and by patient, loving forbearance you will win them over from their foolish departure from their acknowledged standpoint. You are conscious of truth to lean upon, while they have only a manmade creed that will not bear the light of reason, and sooner or later they must see it and acknowledge it.

The denial of the claims of evil and matter is the point that is most disputed and brings the most ridicule; and we must admit that some scientists have aired their newly adopted ideas in a manner so foolish and mystifying to those who do not understand, that many are held back from investigating the subject because they are shocked and mystified by statements that were never explained nor made to seem even rational.

We should not forget that we were all unbelievers till we reached the point where conviction of the truth dawned upon us, and it never dawned upon us by being shocked with foolish statements, neither will it for others.

Let us be "wise as serpents and harmless as doves," and we shall find a way to avoid the fellowship or recognition of evil without shocking any one or showing any discourtesy.

People honestly think it is a falsehood to deny the evils that stand out with such glaring reality to the mortal sense, but some day they will know that it is the falsehood to admit it.

In all the ways and methods known to the civilized world, the efforts to remedy the tendency to evil conditions and search out their causes have all been on a material plane, and it is well known that, upon the whole, there has been no perceptible diminution of evil, and no amelioration of the evil conditions.

The ingenuity of man on a physical plane has never yet discovered a way nor invented a plan by which the errors of the human mind, (with their innumerable bad effects,) could be erased from the boards of his experience; and no matter how talented, how intellectual or how highly educated one may be; no matter how much one may know of material science, such knowledge has never helped men to solve this problem of life, and never will.

Every individual has an equal interest in this great problem of life, if he would only awake to a conscious realization of its importance; but never till now has there been a way clearly opened by which it might be solved. The new light that is thrown upon it by the study of this philosophy is daily proving it the true way. New and higher truths are dawning upon every earnest student of truth daily.

We find that when the conscious mind is willing to be taught, and takes up the line of reasoning regardless of what *seems*, and regardless of all preconceived opinions, and earnestly and firmly, and persistently rejects all falsity by denying the reality of all that is not consistent with the eternal Principle that is God, the diseases and discords, and evil conditions vanish as a reward of his righteous reasoning.

No one need complain that he has no proof of such results following this practice, for there are thousands who are living witnesses, who stand ready to testify to the potency of this saving method; many of them having been miraculously saved and shown the way out of bondage by the process.

But those who stubbornly harden their hearts "will not be persuaded though one rose from the dead." It was even so when Jesus of Nazareth taught them. He quoted the prophecy of Isaiah, saying, "This people's heart is waxed gross, and their ears are dull of hearing, and their eyes they have closed; lest at any time they should see with their eyes, and hear with their ears, and should understand with their hearts, and should be converted and I should heal them."

To be healed is to be saved; the words are from the same root, and no one is made perfectly whole till he is saved from the mortal errors that show forth in sickness.

Every one of ordinary intelligence knows that the world is weary, sick and discouraged with all the recognized systems of cure, as well as those of moral reform and religious training.

The so-called cures do not cure at all.

The moral reforms do not reform at all.

And the religious training in common practice makes either dogmatic bigots and hypocrites, or agnostics and infidels; and each year we see the confidence of the people growing less and less in those recognized systems; we all know there is nothing reliable in them.

We have all repeatedly witnessed the efforts of praying Christians to stay some threatened calamity in the way of pestilence, famine or flood; or perhaps in praying for the life of some highly esteemed dignitary of the church or nation. Have we ever seen those prayers answered? No, never. Such patients have always passed away.

Why is it?

Because they prayed without the righteous conception of God; which, as before stated, is equivalent to praying to a false God.

We read that the "effectual, fervent prayer of the righteous availeth much"; and no matter how fervent and earnest the prayer may be, if it lacks the righteous quality it does not avail. Righteousness means that which is right and true in thought, word and deed.

A true, or righteous conception of God and His laws enables man to offer the effectual prayer, which is the prayer of acknowledgment, of thanksgiving, of affirmation or recognition of what is already provided.

The begging, pleading, beseeching and complaining prayer is never availing.

We can never expect to change the plans or

purposes of God by our pleading, because God is already perfect in wisdom, goodness and love, and His bounty is unlimited ; and He is yesterday, to-day and forever the same.

We must be reconciled to God *as He is;* not God reconciled to us.

The change in apparent conditions that comes by righteous prayer *is in us;* not in God, and this reconciliation can be accomplished in no way but by firmly rejecting, or denying as realities all false ways. Ignore them perfectly, and train the conscious mind to see and know that all that *is*, is good.

This soon brings a realization that what we pray for is already ours.

The affirmation that you have the good you desire, and the acknowledgment of its source with thanksgiving, opens your eyes to the realization of it as already yours; while the complaining, begging and beseeching prayer of one who loves to acknowledge his unworthiness, and loves to tell God how mean and depraved he is, never brings any reward except in an increased sense of unworthiness and depravity.

Such people carry a mental atmosphere wherever they go that causes depression and gloom to every one they meet, and even children shrink from them because of that repellant mental state; and yet they seem so pious.

They generally carry very feeble bodies, and people wonder why such a good man should be so afflicted, and why he is not happier when he is *so good*.

How could he be happy with such false ideas about God and himself?

He *dare* not be happy because he is too unworthy, and he thinks he is pleasing God by being miserable; then he prays to God for release from his misery, and prays with that same foolish error that it is God that afflicts him.

"Therefore the God that ye made you
  Was grievous, and brought you no aid,"
Because it was by your false thought
  "*That the God of your making was made.*"

Every one may be said to make his own God, in the sense that our conception of God *is* God to us; and if our conception is a false one we get no aid by our appeals.

God is Love, and His law is the law of Love, and every one will get the conscious benefit of the law of Love in proportion to his recognition of it, and his acknowledgment of its source with gratitude; which he never can do while his conception of God is so false and he thinks of himself as so separate and apart from God.

We should think of ourselves as spiritual, and in every way the likeness and image of God.

By so realizing our true being we lose that

feeling of base depravity which is so false and depressing, and which is responsible for so many of the physical infirmities and weaknesses that prevail so largely among the piously inclined, according to those old ideas falsely called orthodox.

Such piety seeks debasement and names it humility, instead of seeking to know the true self and naming it the child of God, or the divine self.

Hufeland, a very eminent Prussian who lived a hundred years ago, was physician to the king, and considered very wise and far-seeing in his judgment. He said, that there is a region of man that is never sick, and could not be made sick, and to call that region to reign as the powerful would make the sick man well.

He seemed to have caught a glimpse of the true solution of the health problem; and yet his saying was never made practical in his day, although, like all true thoughts, *it lives*, and has been treasured as a word of wisdom, to be brought forth as a gem of truth when the time was ripe for its appreciation.

All such sayings have their weight, and all such sayings go to prove that this law is as old as time, and might always have blessed the world with immunity from suffering if only men would see and believe the true instead of the false; if only men would use their reason and not judge by appearance in all things.

No one claims to have discovered a new law, and the miracles wrought by the prophets of old are made to seem less a mystery when we know they were the result of their understanding of Divine Law.

Jesus came as the Son of the Most High to teach the power of the word in fulfillment of the law that was from the beginning, and which cannot change because it is the outflow from the eternal Principle, that is God—"The same yesterday, to-day and forever, world without end."

By understanding these principles and proclaiming them as the only power, and recognizing them as the only law, we set them into action.

Many think it a strange proceeding at first because of its simplicity, and because there are no apparent remedies, no appliances, no instruments of torture, by which great ceremony is sometimes made to appear wonderfully wise, but never efficient.

Why should such ceremonious proceedings seem so impressive and important when we never see any good accomplished by them?

When Naaman the leper came in his chariot to the prophet Elisha to be healed of his leprosy, he expected the prophet to perform some strange, mysterious ceremony or incantation to effect a cure; and when the prophet told him to go and wash seven times in Jordan, and made no preparation for other performances, the proud Syrian captain was very angry, and was about to return to his own country without being healed. But his faithful servant remonstrated with him and persuaded him to do as the prophet told him, till he finally yielded and obeyed Elisha, and washed seven times in Jordan, and "Lo, his flesh became like that of a young child."

His haughty pride, and his contempt for the simplicity of the cure had come very near carrying him home *still a leper;* just as pride and contempt for the simplicity of the Christ method of cure in our day causes so many to go through the earth life with such feeble bodies and unhappy states of mind.

In many cases that come for treatment by the Metaphysical Process we find pride and arrogance to be the devils that have to be cast out. In some cases it is hatred and malice; in some it is envy and jealousy; in some it is deceit and treachery, and so on; the catalogue might be extended to great length.

These are the devils that must be cast out; for as long as we entertain them they are our masters, and they hold us in a bondage that must sooner or later be pictured forth in conditions we do not desire.

Even in the case of Naaman, his leprosy was only the sign or picture of the false ways and ungodly passions of the human heart, and it makes no difference in what way it shows forth, whether in leprosy, consumption or whatever, it is the false that shows forth in any case of disease; and the false is what we want to obliterate from our life, whether it is disease of the body, or moral leprosy, the process is the same.

When we effectually deny the error that has caused the infirmity (whatever it may be) we are washing in Jordan. We are stripping off the false beliefs in matter, and evil, and the false power, and making ourselves clean and pure; making ourselves ready for the new garment of health that comes by claiming, affirming, acknowledging the true.

We clothe ourselves with new conditions when we acknowledge God as our health, our strength and our peace.

Health is a state of the mind, insomuch as the conscious mind recognizes truth, and realizes that truth is God, and God is health.

We are not acknowledging God at all when we complain of our pains and diseases, nor when we talk of our burdens, nor when we admit weakness, poverty or misfortune.

If we admit that God is all and in all, how can we turn and declare sickness and pain to be real?

We have seen how the evil passions indulged by the carnal nature, bear fruits in those miserable conditions.

We have seen how anger, hatred, malice, envy, jealousy, deceit and selfishness, bring sorrow, and how the sorrow seems to master mankind. We have seen how the belief in the reality of matter weighs us down and makes us care-burdened and sorrowful; and, as before stated, heretofore no one has ever discovered a way to wipe out these evils; and when every attempt to remedy or better such conditions is met by failure and defeat, and nothing seems to comfort, or cheer, or promise relief, we are assured that God afflicts us for our good, and we must not repine, but look for release only through the portals of death.

We are told with many pious sighs that life is a continual warfare, and there is no hope this side the grave.

How dare the professed followers of Christ teach such a fallacy? So contrary to what the Master taught.

He always talked of the *now*, and never of "beyond the grave;" never.

Is it any wonder that the professing Christians of the age get no answers to their prayers?

Is it any wonder that the problem of life shows

so much confusion with them when they wander so far away from the basic principles they set out with?

Every minister of the gospel that mopes and complains and draws upon his people for sympathy—because of his physical infirmities, his throat troubles, his nervous headaches, his great exhaustion from too much study, or too great a tax upon his strength in his pastoral duties, is a living reproach upon the cause he presumes to represent; and every such condition only advertises his ignorance of gospel truths. Foolishness and ignorance are the devils that hold him in bondage.

No matter how much he may have learned in the great schools of the world, nor with how much pride he may boast of his scholarship; he may attach the M. D. and the D. D., and the L. L. D., and exhaust the alphabet on down to X Y Z for initials to indicate the degrees of learning that have been conferred upon him, and what does it all amount to when he allows himself to be frightened into the pneumonia because he got his feet wet, or because he was exposed to a draught of cold air, or if he thinks he has been exposed to malaria and is stricken with terror at the possible fatal result?

To what purpose has he studied divinity, when

he knows nothing of the dominion that is the inheritance of every child of Divinity?

He finds all those high-sounding titles mere bubbles of empty air when compared with the knowledge of practical truth that is gained by the study of Divinity according to righteous reasoning. He will see that he has begun wrong in his search for knowledge, because first principles have not been mastered first.

As he had not the knowledge of first principles to begin with, his whole course of study is shadowed by that ignorance. The lack of that most essential knowledge appears in everything he attempts.

Although a fine education is a very desirable acquisition, it is still more desirable to begin right.

If first principles are mastered first, all else will be more easily acquired, and the judgment will be educated to detect and discard the false ideas that form so large a part of popular education.

People of great learning are often very poorly educated, and many wise men have discovered so much that is false in the fine education they have spent so much time and money to acquire, and so little that is of practical use, that the world is surfeited with what is called great learning, because it is lacking in knowledge.

It is the false ideas, false impressions and false education that stand in the way of true knowlege, and which have to be rejected by a firm denial of their reality.

The practice of denials, or rejection of error, is the second step toward regeneration; the cleansing process which is so beautifully symbolized by the washing in Jordan.

In this cleansing the mind of error, or casting off the garment of falsehood, we must not leave ourselves empty and naked, else we shall be like the man from whom the evil spirit was cast out; but returned, finding his place empty, swept and garnished; and seeing the emptiness, he took with him seven other devils worse than himself, and they took up their abode with him, making his last state worse than the first.

When we have faithfully cleansed the mind of error by denial, we must not neglect the next step, but clothe ourselves anew with assurances and affirmations of goodness and truth before evil impressions have time to take up their abode again.

The true is always the good, and its character is *positive;* while the false is the *not good*—the evil, which is negative in character. It is equivalent to nothing; hence we deny it.

If you have denied pain, **your** affirmation should be its opposite—*peace, rest, ease.*

Remember always that the good you affirm is of God. If you deny sickness, affirm that God is your health. If you deny weakness, God is your strength. If you deny fear, God is your courage, your peace, your love.

The word you speak or think is the creative agent. The thought or idea is as much *our word* as if spoken, and is even more potent in its effects, because it meets with no opposing argument as it would if given audibly, and, as before stated, every true thought is a word of God.

"Without the word was not anything made that was made."

The true word has power to bring forth whatever we desire in *righteousness*.

Notice, when you affirm that God is your Life, you want to realize that Life is an eternal Principle that nothing can mar or destroy; and that you live, move and have your being in the great ocean of Life; that Life is God; and you are a child of God; one with God, and an heir to eternal Life.

To fully realize this truth is satisfaction. It often brings a conscious thrill of joy that makes you know that Life *must* be unbroken, because its source is eternal and unfailing.

When you continue to realize the allness of God as Life, which shows forth in the ever present good, you feel assured that your denial of the claims of death is righteous reasoning, and you will *stand* by the affirmation that God is the only Life, and you are an heir to eternal Life.

When you affirm that God is Truth and then look about you and see so much that is false, you may be tempted to think that after all, God cannot be omnipresent; but turn from the temptation; it is only the seeming, and never fear to stand by the affirmation, God is Truth—and, There is only God.

In knowing Truth we know God, and thus we lose confidence in the old false ways, and when we affirm that God is Truth, knowing that there is *only God*, the false and troublesome conditions fall away, and we are free. It is then we prove that knowledge of Truth makes us free.

The affirmation, the acknowledgment, makes it manifest; our word has power to prove the law true. Again we repeat the text of the lesson: "Without the word was not anything made that was made."

The most wonderful name of the Father, God, is Love. There is something inexpressible; something indefinable by human language in the Love that is Divine. The Father Love, the Mother Love in One. It asks no reward for its bestowal; it is no respecter of persons; it is the

Holy Spirit, the Mother Principle of the Godhead.

To affirm, "God is Love," and repeat it over and over with trust in your word, is a treatment of itself which has cured many a headache and many a pain that no other remedy could reach.

What more can we ask than perfection, in the character and attributes of the God we worship? And when the Divine Love is bestowed without stint or limit, the least we can do is to acknowledge it with thanksgiving.

"Acknowledge me in all thy ways and I will direct thy paths." It is the honest, sincere realization of the truth we affirm that makes our affirmation potent to bring forth what we desire.

We may attain to that state of mind which will enable us to say as Jesus did, "I and the Father are one," by affirming the Life, Truth and Love of God as Omnipotent, Omniscient and Omnipresent, until we are alive with the realization that it is true.

The Life, Truth and Love are the Father, Son and Holy Spirit, or Mother Principle; the Omnipresent Trinity from which flows constantly the health, strength, wisdom, peace, intelligence, courage and trust; and when we lack any of these desirable qualities in our life, it is because we have not made ourselves one with the Divine

Father, which state of mind clears our perceptions and makes our judgment reliable to consciously know spiritual realities.

God is Substance; the only substance, and when we make this affirmation with understanding we begin to realize the nothingness of all material things. We see how fleeting and illusory are all things that the sight and touch call substantial, and we begin to know that Spirit is the only Substance; the only Reality.

Spirit abideth forever, because Spirit is God. So let us boldly affirm, *God is the only Substance.*

God is the only Intelligence, and knowing this makes us feel that some intelligent force or power unseen, moves us to think and act, whose wisdom is our only source of supply; the great unfailing fountain from which flow unceasing supplies of knowledge.

The boasted human intellect that rears its head with such lofty pride, is but a feeble reflection of the Divine within us, until it is trained to know the real self. And when that is accomplished the Divine self will shine forth, the perfect child expressed in the physical; free from blemish; healthy and strong; happy and free.

This is the heritage of all who find the Divine self.

The greatest wisdom of Greece was expressed

in the two simple words, "Know thyself," carved in stone and placed over the entrance to the Delphic temple.

All great thinkers depreciate the authority of books and Priests, and forms and ceremonies, and aim to know the self.

In every affirmation of good we make with understanding and trust, we are making the true self manifest.

When we say, "God is my Life," knowing that there is no other Life, we begin to realize that the Life that is God, Eternal Life, perfect Life, in which there can be no pain, no disease, no death, nor anything that leads to death, is the Life that is lived within us, pure, free, wise and immortal; we find we are lived by the Divine life.

When the undesirable conditions of pain and sickness come into our lives according to mortal sense, we must know that it is only a human perversion of Divine law, and is not true; hence the need of constant watchfulness in denying the evil that seems so real to mortal sense.

Stand by your basic statements, and all will be well.

You see how easy it is to take up this line of thought and follow on with pure reasoning.

If God is the only Life, Substance and Reality, and God is Spirit, Omnipresent, then you say,

I am Spirit, because I am the offspring of Spirit; I am Mind, because I am the idea, the likeness and image of Omnipotent Mind; I live, move and have my being in omnipresent Wisdom and Love.

The very thinking of such thoughts, or speaking such words with understanding takes away all burdens, all fear and anxiety; we feel that truly we have a Father and friend who cares for us in love, whose power is unlimited, and we trust Him, knowing His law is love and mercy.

To give yourself such discipline daily soon brings the assurance that through you the power of righteous thought may work for the uplifting of others, and you set it into action by speaking the true word; by acknowledging the allness of the good; and you will feel a certain conviction that a healing potency, a comforting influence goes out from you to reach with health or cheer the one to whom you send it; and you always find your good words return to bless and strengthen you.

Nowhere else is found such rest, such peace, such relief from burdens; and in no other way can the Divine Love that heals the hurt be brought so near and made so comforting,

In no other way has freedom been made so tangible and sure.

By no other means has the **prophecy in Reve-**

lation been explained. We see clearly how it can be brought to pass in every single life.

It says, "There shall be no more pain, neither sorrow nor crying, for former things have passed away, and behold, all things have become new."

And this is the literal fulfillment of the prophecy in every individual case that is willing to abide by the requirements; but there is no promise without some condition to be met.

Isaiah said, "They that wait upon the Lord shall renew their strength."

To wait upon the Lord is to trust the law of God.

Solomon said, "In the way of righteousness is life; and in the pathway thereof *there is no death.*"

Jesus said, "If a man keep my sayings he shall never see death." Also, "If ye abide in me, and my words abide in you, ye shall ask what ye will, and it shall be done unto you."

The conditions to be met may all be summed up in the one word, "*Overcome.*"

In the denial of evil you overcome evil conditions.

"To him that overcometh I will give of the tree of life."

"To him that overcometh I will give to eat of the hidden manna."

"To him that overcometh will I give power over nations."

"He that overcometh shall inherit all things."

The only sure way to overcome the universal beliefs in evil and in the power of evil, is to take the following Statement of Being with the denials attached, and make it a religious duty to give yourself this discipline daily, once, twice or three times, as you find it convenient.

Take it in sections at first, and thoroughly familiarize yourself with every statement and denial; always giving your affirmations of good after making your denials. For every denial of evil, you should affirm its opposite good; always acknowledging God in the good you affirm.

God is my health.

God is my strength.

God is my wisdom.

SELF-DISCIPLINE.

There is but one Substance, one Power, one Intelligence, one Life, one Truth, one Love, which is the one God of the Universe, who is Spirit, the all good which fills all space. God is omnipresent good.

I am a child of God, "made in His image, after His likeness."

I also am Spirit, I live, move and have my being in God; and as I am like my Father I cannot be sick, nor suffer pain, and no evil can come to me because all that *is*, is good.

I deny the reality of evil, I deny the power of evil, I deny the reality of pain, of sorrow, of sickness, of weakness, of weariness, of poverty, of misfortune, of discouragement, of fear, of doubt, of foolishness, of ignorance, of discord, of danger, of death, and of all evil influences from every source, because all evil is false.

I declare there is no power in any mortal law to hold me in bondage. Lust and sensuality of any shade or degree have no power to harm me. Deceitfulness, treachery, lying or hypocrisy are powerless to affect me for evil. There is no power in calumny, suspicion, criticism or censure. There is no power in anger or ill temper, or scorn, or contempt; there is no power in prejudice or superstition. There is no power in selfishness, envy, jealousy, pride, hatred, malice or revenge.

I am law against all that is false and foolish, and I declare the influence of all such passions utterly null and void to me. I declare all such passions powerless to harm *any one*.

I also deny the reality of matter, because God is the only Substance, and God is Spirit.

I also deny that the appearance we call matter has any Life, Substance or Intelligence, because God is the only Life and Intelligence, and God is Spirit.

Only the Good is true; only the Good has power. God is health. God is Stength. God is Wisdom. God is Peace.

Affirm whatever good you desire as of God *always*. It is the prayer of acknowledgment, the prayer of thanksgiving.

To "pray without ceasing and in everything give thanks," is the prayer of affirmation. Say to yourself after each practice of your discipline, "My word shall not pass away, nor return to me void; it shall accomplish that whereunto it is sent."

CASE OF HEALING.

A lady came to us who had been for years suffering with what physicians call eczema of the lower limbs. Every remedy known to Materia Medica had been tried with no relief whatever. Her limbs from the knee to the feet were swollen out of all resemblance to the human leg, and the ichorous exudation, together with the itching and burning, was intolerable.

In addition to this torture from eczema she was subject to very severe and prolonged attacks of nervous headache. She was treated by science about five days, during which time she entered the class and discontinued the treatments.

Before the close of the course of lessons her limbs were reduced to their natural size and symmetry and every vestige of humor had disappeared, the skin healed as smooth and healthy as that of a child; the headaches had completely disappeared, and now after three years' experience in the science she testifies to a continuance of perfect health and peace. She said, "I never before realized what the promise meant to those who hunger and thirst after righteousness." Besides the feeling of perfect security against all sickness herself, she helps and heals others and lives a life of continual praise and thanksgiving for the blessed knowledge of this truth.

LESSON IV.

"As the body without the spirit is dead, so faith without works is dead also:"

WHEN a student of truth begins to realize the power there is in true words, he naturally feels a desire to talk about it and tell his friends what marvelous changes have come to him in health, in peace, or in circumstances, from using the scientific mental arguments given in the second and third lessons.

We all feel this desire to share our new-found joys with our friends when these great truths first dawn upon us, and it is good for us to feel the desire. At the same time we would caution every student for their own peace of mind not to be too eager.

Until you are more familiar with the principles, perhaps your ability to explain your position is not equal to your zeal in wanting your friends to know the beautiful gospel of health and peace you have found; and it is wise to keep silent about the process by which you train your mind in the knowledge of truth, until you feel able to answer all questions that arise.

Your friends will argue of course from the old standpoint, and unless you are well grounded in what you know, you may be easily confused, and things may begin to look more rational from that old standpoint again; and you will wonder if after all you are not mistaken about this new Science.

The old way of reasoning from the evidence of the senses, appeals *too* strongly to the conscious mind for us to be convinced without some misgivings; and the argument from the carnal side is liable to get the upper hand unless you are soundly anchored in the truth.

In view of this we advise students to refrain from all controversy regarding the truth or falsity of Science, until you can give clear and convincing reasons for the claims of Science.

All controversy tends to discord, and discord is not scientific. Harmony is the law of the universe, and whatever disturbs the harmony is error.

Those who oppose and dispute the claims of the Science, do so on grounds purely material, and have no conception at all of the higher spiritual law, and still less belief in the possibility of the human intellect being trained to grasp what to them has always been called the supernatural. If convinced of the truth in one point, they will always find *another* point to attack, which *to them* seems weak.

It has been an old and commonly accepted idea among orthodox Christians to look upon all science as antagonistic to religion; and while that idea has been abandoned by the more liberal and advanced thinkers, there are still *too many* who look upon Science as dangerously heterodox, not realizing that a science must of necessity spring from principles that are true, else it would not be Science; also that all true principles are of God, therefore any *true* religion must be scientific.

That which distinguishes the *Science of Mind* from the cold material sciences of mathematics, chemistry, astronomy, etc., is the predominence of the love principle, which heals, comforts, and blesses. The material sciences may very reasonably be called divinely true, because they are based upon true principles, and yet they lack the Life and Love that rounds out the complete Science of all sciences, which embraces *all* truth, and which will serve the race in the solution of every problem when people fully comprehend that the gospel of Christ is scientific.

Science, from the word *Scire*, means *to know;* and any true principles or combination of truths, arranged in orderly fashion, so as to admit of demonstration, may be called a science.

Christ, from the ancient word Krestos, means Truth. Your clergymen very likely will tell you that Christ means, "the anointed," and he will go no further with an explanation, because it is the custom of theologians to be satisfied with that; but the word means truth, and the one who represents or embodies the principle of truth is the anointed one.

It has been a custom among the Jews since the days of Aaron and Moses, for the high priests to be anointed with oil. The high priest is supposed to be a teacher of religious truth—and the anointing with oil is a very solemn religious ceremony among the Jews.

Jesus was the embodiment of truth in the flesh, hence he was called Christ—the anointed.

The world has always called those who were anointed to preach the truth, "*the Christ.*"

Gautama Buddha was the Christ of the Buddhists; so also was Confucius considered the Christ, but none of the so-called Christs have taught absolute truth unmixed with error, except Jesus. He only among them all, spoke, and taught, and lived, and proved the unerring truth; and what could be more fitting than that those who follow his teachings and practices, and demonstrate over error as he did, should give his name to the science that explains the principles he taught, which *none* of these objectors do.

Truth as he taught it is found to be a living principle, and by the knowledge of truth, we set the principle into action.

When set into action by understanding it, its tendency is always to life.

Jesus said to keep his words would make us one with eternal life.

To keep his words means, to keep their true meaning in the mind, and to square our lives by the principles he taught.

The words of no other teacher will do this; not even those who were called the Christ, because their teachings were not always true.

In every instance where they taught a truth, it was in perfect harmony with what Jesus taught, but so much error was mixed with what they taught that the tendency was more toward death than to life.

If such men as Plato, Aristotle, Milton. Shakespeare, and many others, had only taught absolute truth instead of mixing such glittering falsities with their brilliant ideas, with what grand results they might have used their powers to lift men out of the bondage of evil.

Although their ideas may give polish to the human intellect, they do not inspire the soul to reach above the plane of mere human intellect, except when they strike a note of pure truth, and in those gems of true thought *only* are men made better by their having lived.

The search for the laws of life can never be successful on a material plane.

There is a law well known among true philosophers, by which we learn that people grow to be like what they study most earnestly, and think most about, and the more absorbingly one devotes himself to any theme, the more he takes on the character of that study in his physical life.

In ancient times there were schools for the study of Divine law, and students who were faithful and diligent accomplished wonderful things by the study.

The study of Divinity is the study of "First Cause"—the study of God, and the earnest, faithful student of Divine law, cannot fail to discover his powers as a child of God, and as he daily realizes more and more his own divine nature, he becomes more and more God-like in his life, and in his power over all his environments, and he finds that he truly has dominion over all things, and may put all difficulties under his feet.

Those ancient students of Divine law, who were most faithful and devout, acquired such proficiency in the knowledge of true principles as to become the acknowledged prophets; and their achievements in the line of healing and performing miracles, were truly God-like.

It was only by a knowledge of these principles that Elisha, and Joshua, and Daniel and many others (who were called the holy men of Israel), were able to defy natural law and make the law of Spirit work for them. We find that even now, with a knowledge of this wonderful law of mind, any one may know and use the same law, so far as he is willing to discard the old errors that hang like a veil between his conscious mind and the truth that would enlighten it.

If we want to be Christ-like, we must study and accept the principles Christ taught. If we want to be God like, let us study the mystery of Godliness.

Jesus taught this Divine law with such simplicity that the only marvel is, that students of his gospel have failed so utterly in understanding the principles he taught.

This lack of understanding explains the lack of Christ-like powers, and Christ-like deeds among his professed followers.

Where do we find any students of Divinity, in this age, who have so mastered the principles of Divine law, as to be able to prophesy, or perform miracles, or heal the sick?

They are often very diligent in the study of man-made creeds instead; or as Jesus said to the Scribes and Pharisees, "In vain do they worship *me*, while teaching for doctrine the commandments of men."

And have not such teachings proved "*in vain*"?

Now, we do not want to attach to a true Science, any of those old false and foolish doctrines or dogmas that blind us to what is real and true, but we want to hold fast to all that is true, and thus increase our confidence in the power of truth to set us free.

Ask yourself, Did it ever make me love God, or fill me with an earnest desire to serve Him better, by believing that He created me totally wicked and depraved?

Does it make me love to serve God better by believing that He sets a personal devil to follow me in all my ways; to deceive and tempt me to do and act contrary to His commands?

Does it increase my confidence in the power of God to believe in another great power opposed to God in all things?

Have any of these beliefs ever brought me peace of mind, or health of body?

To ask yourself these questions with a sincere desire to be set in the way of truth, you are compelled to answer, " No. None of these beliefs has ever helped me to find the divinity within me, or lift me out of bondage."

Now, to study Christ in the *spirit of Christ*, will lift you out of bondage.

If we keep His sayings our lofty purposes and righteous desires intensify daily, and the living truth thrills all our being with certainty of eternal life; we feel ourselves to be one with the deathless Christ Himself.

In the teachings of Christ, there is no belief in evil to weigh us down, no belief in sickness, no belief in death; but the living Christ (Truth) shall reign from sea to sea, and from the rivers to the uttermost parts of the earth; loosing the coils of the world's belief in evil, till all the children of earth are redeemed by the Christ's teachings, by the absolute truth understood.

Notice, the Christ (Truth) has always been with us, but not being understood, it has not made us consciously free; we are not fully redeemed till we fully recognize the power of truth, and acknowledge the freedom.

The law works by orderly processes, the same as the laws of chemistry, or mathematics, both of which are simply a shadowing forth of the spiritual law.

In the study of *any* science and all sciences, the steps are orderly and sequential; that is, one step follows another in the regular order necessary to school the mind to an understanding of the principles taught.

In changing the beliefs of the mind (which in some cases amounts to complete revolution) it is accomplished by a new line of thought, or an *entirely* new set of arguments.

When we grasp the full perception of the argument, as some do in one grand flash of illumination, the clouds of darkness and doubt are lifted at once, which experience will not come while the mind still opposes and objects and questions every step of the way; for this reason the mental change from ignorance to knowledge is slow to most of us, because most of us do question and doubt at first; and yet the change that comes slowly is as a rule more satisfying to the reasoning mind, because one is better able to explain the process of passing from darkness to light, or from ignorance to knowledge; we can give a better reason for the hope within us when we have deliberately reasoned it out.

It has always been the aim of philanthropist and preacher and teacher through all the ages to teach what would most benefit the race; but all have failed to define the distinction most important to know between the spiritual and the material—the mortal and the immortal; and yet in moments of apparent inspiration, when the highest truths have seemed to dawn upon them, they all very strangely seem to agree, and will utter the same truths, *in substance*.

It could not be otherwise when all inspiration comes from the one great Intelligence.

Herein lies the science of Christianity. No

statements of true Christian principles can by any possibility conflict, and every truth will agree with every other truth.

Science is science and all true calculations that start from a true basis, must of necessity bring results that are true; whether in mathematics, astronomy, or the problem of life.

If we set out in this problem of life on the basis that Spirit is the only Substance, we must calculate all the way along in harmony with that statement. We build the world about us as we think, and as we think so we believe.

Thinking and wording do the building. The word is Spirit; that is, the essence of the word is the spirit of it. "He sent his word and healed them."

When He sends His word He sends by a messenger; we are the messengers, and it is the "God that worketh in you, both to will and to do of His good pleasure."

The healing word is sent in the Divine law that erases the false effects of mortal error, and this Divine law must be acknowledged as the only power before it will act.

You begin your acknowledgment of this law when you declare that, "Spirit is the only substance," and if all your thoughts and ideas harmonize with this first statement of science, you will begin to build your world harmoniously around you.

If to-day you rise to the full realization that sickness, pain and sorrow are a delusion, of course you reject them, you denounce them as errors that you will have no more fellowship with, and you realize health and peace from your reasoning. You are building harmonious conditions around you.

Then to-morrow you forget all about this lofty state of mind that gave you such peace and comfort, and you begin to think and talk of sickness and pain again, and recall all the miserable conditions you suffered as if they were an actual reality; your words and thoughts are taking on the old errors again, and you are rewarded by a return of the sickness and pain. You have unintentionally forgotten that "thinking and wording do the building."

Then you are apt to think that the science doesn't work for you as it does for others, or as you expected it to do, and by that thought you are sending out clouds of darkness that hide the truth from others, as well as yourself.

"By thy words thou art justified, and by thy words thou art condemned."

"Only the good is true," and when you have once proved it so, stand by the statement, and make all things bend to it.

All evil of whatever character is simply negation, nonentity, nothingness.

All the ancient philosophers who are quoted as so wise and wonderful, declare in substance that "all evil is negation, and all matter is delusion, and that we take what *only seems* for the reality.

The Scriptures tell us that God made all that *is*, and that He made all things good; they tell us also that He *knows all things*, and looks upon all He has created as perfect, and that He is too pure to behold iniquity or sin. Then of course sin and iniquity are not a reality; what seems so is *mortal mind's invention;* a delusion that bears the same relation to our higher nature, that the hideous nightmare does to the conscious mind when we awake.

When the conscious mind allows the senses to rule in its reports of evil and pain, it has wandered away from true principles, and it suffers the consequence in this seeming condition of pain, which is typified by the prodigal son who wandered away from his father's house and took up his abode in a far country. The far country is the false state of mind in which we are only conscious of what the carnal nature sees.

When the prodigal son began to suffer want "he came to himself," and said, "I will arise and go to my Father."

When the conscious mind begins to realize the fact that all pain and discord are the result of foolishly depending on what the senses tell us, it begins to come to itself and remember the comfort and peace it once enjoyed before wandering away into this far country, or this false way of thinking, and it says, "I will arise and return to true principles."

The coming to itself is when it realizes how false the mortal way is; and the turning from the false to the true is the return to the Father's house, where all is joy and gladness.

The beautiful lesson taught by this parable shows how surely we all may find the true way if we will. Try and forget the old false conception of this lesson, which places all the benefits of obedience away off in the world to come, and know that here and now are all the blessings we desire, if only we will see the true way to obtain them.

The Psalmist David said, "Only with thine eyes shalt thou behold and see the reward of the wicked." He meant only with the eyes of flesh, of course. Spiritual perception knows only goodness, while mortal mind judges by appearance.

To judge by appearance, we should pronounce the child of the universal Father often very imperfect; often sick and miserable; he would seem (in many cases) to be the creation of a being capable of making a great deal of wretchedness; but science denies this, and as science deals with principles, it makes man by pure reasoning to be the creation of a Being whose very attributes preclude the possibility of His making *anything* imperfect.

How could He make His own children totally depraved when by His own Infinite perfection He could have no such conception as depravity?

What a monstrous perversion is the doctrine of total depravity; and who can estimate the wickedness and infidelity it has caused?

Of all things created, man is God's masterpiece; the image and likeness of Himself.

He called all mankind His children, and pronounced all He had created, "*very good.*"

"Come, and let us reason together," respecting these things.

We find that man in his essential nature is the spiritual likeness and image of God or the idea of God; while the physical man is but the unreal shadow of the Divine idea, or the outward expression of the thoughts and beliefs of the finite mind.

To reason thus, makes us consciously one with the mind that creates; and until we realize this oneness, we are wanderers in the far country of mortal error.

When Kepler discovered the perfection of the law of planetary motion and distance, like one inspired, he caught the idea of unvarying law, and cried out, "Oh, God! I think thy thoughts after thee."

Unvarying law makes it utterly impossible for an all-wise Creator, whose very attributes are perfection, to create a being in His own likeness and image that is imperfect and miserable; therefore the miserable appearance is the delusion of mortal sense, or the invention of the carnal man, and nothing but the word of truth will dispel the delusion.

The power of the word has to be continually kept in mind while the student of truth pursues the study, because it is the word that creates.

The Saviour said, "My words are Spirit and they are Life." And He said, that for us to keep His words would make us one with eternal Life.

Now to keep the spirit of his words, we must reject all that does not agree with his teachings. So with the words of denial we open the door to freedom; we have been in bondage to error, and we wrench asunder the chains of ignorance that have bound us to shadows, by our word of denial.

This experience is often like a revelation, because it is a truth that comes to our knowledge by earnestly seeking wisdom from the source of all truth and wisdom.

It is also by our *true word* that we gather courage and assurance when we affirm the good. The inner man perceives and knows what the natural man cannot comprehend.

We feel a conscious thrill of freedom that amounts to knowing the absolute nothingness of pain and misery, and a certainty that we have dominion over such conditions.

We see that all misery and wretchedness are the out-showing of erroneous reasoning, and that all such reasoning lacks foundation.

We look back upon the bitter experiences of the past as a miserable dream.

We see how falsely—how needlessly we suffered in those beliefs, and how our foolish false beliefs augmented our miseries.

We learn that thoughts are words which make up our happiness or misery, and that thoughts can be controlled; and then we find it reasonable to say, if we control our thoughts aright, we shall show forth right conditions.

According to appearance, the conscious mind would say that circumstances and conditions control our thoughts; but according to righteous reasoning our thoughts should control circumstances and conditions. We must make them do it.

To accept the appearance for the reality is to remain in bondage to ignorance. We prove our ignorance of the laws of mind when we give up our dominion to mortality's claims.

What we know of the effect of silent thought proves thought to be the first active agent in all things.

Thought first suggests the idea of sickness, and immediately sets about some invention for a name, and it is thought that decides to name it after some popular belief of mortal mind; then it is thought that suggests the remedy.

We first think of the soothing character of an opiate before the opiate is given, and we don't know that the opiate is but a symbol of the thought that suggests it; we don't know that to turn the thought from the material drug to spiritual truth will heal the patient quicker and better without the opiate; so we proceed in our ignorance and give the symbol, perfectly oblivious of the potency of true thoughts or true words to heal.

The same error obtains among such Christians as depend upon the sacraments to give spiritual comfort, instead of relying upon the true word which the sacraments only symbolize.

The body and blood of Jesus Christ are of themselves but a symbol of His word; and the bread and wine are but symbols of the symbol, and can only satisfy as mortal mind believes in it, or as the Catholic devotee believes in the efficacy of the holy water.

In case of sickness, we bring quicker and more permanent cure every time by the true word or thought, than we can with the drug, and it is a remedy that is always at hand; if we are sufficiently in earnest to keep the mind in the way of truth; then there are no nauseating bottles and pills and powders to handle, and no instruments of torture; no blisters to dress; no greasy ointments; no unpleasant odors, but just the clean, pure word of truth that corrects the foolish, false beliefs and makes health shine forth.

We may very reasonably look forward to the time when it will be a mark of reproach as well as ignorance for any one to be sick; when the knowledge of truth will cover the earth as the waters cover the sea." Then there will be no sickness to cure, because the great numbers who think only truth will become great health and strength centers from which there will constantly radiate health, strength, peace and harmony, and their light will so shine as to convince the world of the reality of the truth they live.

When we consider how young the science is, and the scoffs and skepticism it meets with, we need not wonder that many who embrace it are weak and incompetent in their efforts at first. It takes a brave heart to bear the ridicule and criticism so freely lavished by the world (even if it is in ignorance), and many allow it to overcome, and the science is held responsible for their failures, while in truth their failures were due to the *lack* of science.

We all begin our work of healing with fear and trembling, and we are beset with many doubts of our ability to heal *at all*, until we become more thoroughly grounded in the knowledge by practice and experience; each *little* victory is worth a great deal to the novice until courage and confidence are established.

All failure to cure is a sign of fear; and fear is sign of doubt in the power of truth to do; and doubt betrays the lack of thorough understanding of the principles on which the healing argument is based.

We need to rise *above* all criticism, and above ridicule or unfavorable comment, to where we can truly say, "*None of these things move me.*"

People very soon learn to respect the stand one takes when he shows that it is taken on principle, and that nothing can move him from it.

We desire to see every student of truth so thoroughly trained in the understanding of these principles that no argument, no ridicule, no opposition or persecution can move him; and so firm that "the gates of hell shall not prevail against his thoughts."

This is the same truth that Jesus said to Peter was the rock upon which he should build his church, "and the gates of hell should not prevail against it."

The gates of hell are the assaults of opposition, calumny, persecution, and misrepresentation, that have always been hurled at faithful followers of truth.

And the false doctrines and half-hearted service of professing Christians may also be called the gates of hell. All things that tend to shut out the whole blessed helpful truths of the gospel of Christ, are gates of hell.

God said, "Let there be a firmament in the midst of the waters." We are taught that this passage signifies, "Let there be a firm mind."

As before explained, "waters" signify or symbolize the conscious mind that is ever changing and drifting and surging here and there like the waves of the sea; and "firmament" means a firm mind; or, Let there be a steadfast certainty as to what you know; let there be no wavering or doubt or hesitation, but base your position upon true Principle, and then *stand*.

This steadfast certainty of truth can be established in every mind by the faithful practice of affirmations, after the denial of all error has been thoroughly done.

Nothing so inspires hope, confidence and courage as to faithfully and trustfully affirm the good things provided us, as already ours.

We begin to feel that we have the key that unlocks the storehouse of wisdom and bounty, and the problem of life seems much nearer being solved, and our enthusiasm is sometimes unspeakable.

But we must go through the trial of our faith; no one escapes this trial, though the faithful need suffer nothing.

We find the ways of the world still opposed to the ways of science, and we find ourselves exposed to many rebuffs, sometimes our dearest friends turn against us just as Jesus said they would. Sometimes we are left completely alone among skeptics and the most merciless of scoffers; in fact, everything tends to discourage and depress, as it seems to mortal sense, and then is the time to show your faith in the principles you have espoused.

Then is the time to prove your principles true. "Let there be a firm mind." Show to the world that you have taken a firm and definite stand by principles that will bear you out, and you will prove it to them.

The cleansing by denials, and the spiritualizing and comforting practice of affirmations are only a beginning.

We have to stand porter at the door of conscious thought continually, to keep down the deceptions of mortality's claims.

We are constantly meeting with strong sense evidence that contradicts *our* statements; all we see, all we hear, and even the popular learning of the land are opposed to our statements, and the cruel sneers of the cold, heartless world begin to shake our confidence in our own ability to withstand so much; *then* we think of the grand principles that we *know* are true, and all this array of discouragements sinks into insignificance, and we are stronger for the trial.

Every student of truth will sooner or later have all these phases of discouragement to contend with, and "blessed is he that overcometh."

Everything we see, and even all nature seems arrayed against us, if we judge by appearance. When the senses corroborate what the skeptics say, we are apt to think the science is in danger till we remember that we are not to judge by appearance.

Never mind what seems at all. According to

pure reason, science is true; according to appearance it is not true, and you have to choose either the truth that *is*—or the error that only *seems*.

Doubt grows spontaneously in mortal mind and needs no cultivation, but the strangest fact is that we are not inclined to doubt the false at all; that seems more real than all else; but we doubt the *true*, and generally refuse to believe it till it is proven.

"Blessed are they that have not seen and yet *have* believed."

All these temptations to return to the old ways are strengtheners, if we turn them to account.

"It is the trial of your faith which worketh patience, and patience Godliness, and Godliness the peaceable fruits of righteousness," which means the result of right thinking.

When such discouraging experiences come, as they are very liable to do, go back to your self-training and regain your peace of mind as if just beginning; and until your perceptions are clear and sure, and sufficiently developed to solve your life problem without wavering, you will need to use the rule we give you, till it *is* accomplished.

You want to feel and affirm that God works through you to will and to do, and you want to know that whenever you are prompted to do a good deed it is God working in you, and you have virtually surrendered your human will to the Divine, which works through you; and as long as you leave *self* out of the question the Divine will work *for* you, and *through* you, and *in* you, and thus you make the divinity within you manifest; not only in works, but in the physical expression.

The finding of the real self is the work of the conscious mind under the willing guidance of Divine Wisdom. It is a process of unfoldment which is accomplished only by the study of God or the Good as the Supreme Principle of the universe, with which we are inseparably connected in spirit.

We find the *true* self only when we utterly deny the mortal self and its claims.

The very corner stone, or foundation of this practice is,. first, in the proper understanding of what you are to deny, why you deny it, when you deny certain errors for certain conditions, and in what manner you do it to make it effectual; then in following up the denials with such affirmations as are most needed in the case, with perfect confidence and trust in the law, and perfect confidence and trust in this proceeding as a means of setting the law into action.

This course of procedure, either in self-discipline, or in treating others, is what brings the kingdom of heaven, because it tears away the veil that hides the Divine Self. When the kingdom of heaven is made manifest is "when the without is as the within," or when the Divine Self shines forth in perfect health, a reflection of the Divine Image.

CURE OF ASTHMA.

A middle aged lady who had suffered from childhood with asthma in its most distressing form, with most exhausting and frequent paroxysms of coughing, in addition to which was a palsied condition of the hands, arms and head, by which she was deprived of using a pen or pencil, was cured by these lessons and a few treatments. Of course she had been through the usual experience with physicians all to no purpose, as after years of experimenting all agreed that nothing could be done for her.

After the first treatment she sat through the lesson with only two slight paroxysms of coughing, and went home very much cheered. After the second treatment she sat through the lesson without coughing at all. After the third treatment and lesson she declared she was healed, and from that time on she walked several blocks to the class and home again after the lesson, while at first she had to be assisted from the carriage to the class room.

About the sixth lesson she brought pencil and book and astonished her friends by taking notes and writing nearly as steadily and rapidly as other students.

Her cough was gone. She breathed like other people, and her hands had ceased to tremble.

Never was more grateful joy expressed by a healed patient than by her. Even her looks proclaimed the praise that was in her heart.

LESSON V.

"Be ye therefore perfect as your Father which is in heaven is perfect."

EVERY child of God shows forth three phases of enlightenment to the conscious mind; the religious, the philosophical, the scientific.

The religious is the ultimate, the highest, because it is that which binds us to the great First Cause, the Father, God.

It is an interior perception of truth, or knowledge of true principles, and a willing obedience to their promptings.

The phase of the mind we call philosophical is simply the point where the conscious mind reasons from an intellectual standpoint only, and before it reaches the interior perception or spiritual illumination, and yet has a clear intellectual perception as to how principles work; and by a close adherence to the philosophical reasoning we find we can prove things in such a manner as to call it a science.

A scientific truth is the same as Divine Law reduced to the understanding of the human intellect; for a thing cannot be scientific unless it is based upon a true foundation.

Truth is God, and Divine Law is the law of God.

True science points the way to true philosophy, and philosophy according to true science, leads to religion, and religion to God.

Each is necessary to the other.

A religious statement is often very obscure until philosophy reduces it to the comprehension of the intellect, and then science steps in and proves it by demonstration.

Thus we see how religion, philosophy and science strengthen each other. How each one is dependent upon the others, and neither is complete and perfect without the others.

There is a true and philosophical reason for all the statements of the Christ Science, else it would not be scientific; and as the statements prove true, they must finally be known and acknowledged of all men as the only rational way of proving our sonship; the *re* and *ligo* that binds us to God and makes us conscious of our divine inheritance.

It is by philosophical reasoning according to this Divine Science that we discover how every mind is possessed of the faculty of radiating its quality, or diffusing an influence corresponding to its character, which influence reaches every other mind that is found open and receptive to that influence; especially when near or in any way associated.

Any observing person will readily notice the difference in the influence sent out by the different qualities of mind.

When you see a person who is timid, undecided and vacillating, never having any decision of character, or judgment of his own, you may be sure that such a mind is acting under some influence that produces this lack of judgment; he is acting under authority, although he may not be aware of it.

He is unconsciously moved by some mind that holds an idea of superiority over him, which seems to deprive him of wisdom and judgment to act for himself; at the same time the mind that assumes superiority over him may also be acting under authority.

He may be very learned and scholarly, and yet allow the conclusions of other men to imprison him and harness him down to such ideas and theories as are found in the books written by great men, and he is proud of his great learning, pedantic and conceited, and his mental presence completely extinguishes all originality in those who do not hold themselves above such mental influence.

The books written by the so-called great men of the world, often contain ideas as false in principle and theory as the ideas of the uneducated; and if written by one of strong will and firm personal influence, that influence is felt even by the reader of the book, and no true education is possible by depending upon such authority.

The only true education is gained by such teaching as tends to the drawing forth of what is within, and enlarging our powers by a knowledge of our Divine ability to judge of men and principles, regardless of all human authority.

"He that is spiritual judgeth all things, yet he himself is judged of no man."

It is not always those who have the greatest learning that are the best educated.

We send our children to schools where they are taught a great deal about the stars and the planets and their distances, and their atmospheres, all about the rocks and minerals, all about the different monarchs that have governed the different nations, and all about the wars and the great quarrels between nations; and they are taught ways and methods of becoming great generals and mighty warriors, with the impression deeply rooted and grounded, that these are the things that make up the best good in life; or that the acquirement of great wealth will best satisfy their aspirations; or that political power and great influence in government affairs would make great men of them; all these mistakes of education are *now* at this very time bearing fruit in the restless lives and wretched bodily conditions, and discontent from unholy ambitions so common in every community.

Why are our insane asylums so overcrowded with unfortunate lunatics? Why are so many suicides recorded in every morning paper? Why do so many succumb to the fatal belief in softening of the brain? And of paralysis, and apoplexy?

All because of false education in one way or another.

Many of the physical troubles so prevalent in this age are superinduced by the great competition, or by an unlawful ambition to excel in whatever is undertaken, even to the disadvantage and destruction of others.

In politics, and in seeking power and place in government affairs, a man scarcely considers the position worth having unless it is gained by the complete ruin and overthrow of his opponent, who may be more worthy than himself.

In business matters it is *very little* better, and in the professions, especially with the medical profession, all is confusion and discord in the struggle for supremacy. Even with clergymen this ambition is often deplorably manifest. It really begins with children in the schoolroom, and grows more intense with each year, and is so often encouraged by the parents that many have been called upon to mourn the untimely death of the promising son or daughter.

This destroying ambition is not confined to the male portion of mankind, by any means.

It permeates every phase and grade of society. It is the bane of fashionable life. It creates jealousies and animosities, and engenders so much strife over the non-essentials of life, that its degrading influence *morally* can scarcely be estimated, to say nothing of its destructive influence upon the physical.

When people are stricken with physical maladies they never dream that it is due to such false ideas of life; and hundreds may sicken and die from such causes, and the world jogs on as before, enacting the same foolish drama year after year, creating more lunatics and providing more convicts for the prisons, and more sorrow for the honest and level-headed that escape such influences.

The world has never till now been awake to the fact that all the prevailing diseases of the world may be traced to such causes, and in every case has its origin in the false influences exerted over the people—beginning with the young minds that are so plastic to every strong wave of thought, and extending through every community and to every individual in the community.

If any one presumes to set up an opinion not in harmony with the popular beliefs, he is set aside as a little strange, or a little *off;* consequently truth has to wait patiently for the recognition that has to be made before it will serve us.

Truth can afford to wait; and if truth were human instead of Divine, how it would smile to see the eager scramble of men after shadows, and the reluctance with which they often accept the substance.

The mental influence exerted in every case is good or bad, according to the quality of the dominent minds, and besides the quality and character of the mental influence sent out by all minds, even the secret opinions and beliefs they hold are more or less felt.

The strongest effect produced by opinions and beliefs is in our views concerning life—its source, its origin and purpose.

We throw light or shade over others according as we think truly or falsely of God and His dealings with us as His children.

Who does not remember in childhood the feeling of gloom and depression experienced, whenever the minister made his pastoral visits; especially if he happened to be of the persuasion that believe in the doctrine of reprobation and eternal damnation for infants and heathen? His visits were always like a funeral occasion, and always left a gloom over the home like the shadow of some great sorrow.

We used to suppose it was his extreme goodness which gave us such a sense of unworthiness and actual depravity in his presence; and yet we did not know of any wickedness we had been guilty of; we only knew that we felt terribly wicked and depraved whenever he came, and those feelings never troubled us at other times.

We mention this to show the effect of such false ways of thinking.

The very presence of such a mind seems to emit a poisonous quality to the atmosphere we breathe, and such pastoral visits never leave any cheer or hope behind, and no one is the better for his call.

His sermons were generally about the wrath of God and the danger of impenitence and the awful doom awaiting the sinner, but never of the love of God, and after his solemn visits God seemed more angry than ever.

The depressing influence such a mind sends out is all due to the monstrous false conception of God; and his opinions regarding Divine law were of the same monstrous character, therefore he could only radiate darkness and gloom. It is the law.

The very opposite effect is produced by coming in contact with one who holds absolutely true views concerning God. He diffuses love and harmony wherever he goes; his presence is like sunshine, and his visits are alive with hope and courage. There is cheer in the very thought of his coming, as well as in the memory of his genial presence.

The first is sad and sorrowful over the afflictions that he thinks God has sent upon his children, and he believes that they must submit to the punishment because it is the will of God; he seems to live in constant fear of being elected to eternal perdition, and he goes about with his sad forebodings in his face, and in every move, and thus emits darkness and envelopes every one in it who comes within his influence.

The other is bright and cheery because he knows that God is a loving Father who bestows bounteous blessings upon His children without stint. He knows that God imparts life, health, strength and vigor, simply for the acknowledgment, and with this confidence and trust there is nothing to be sad and sorrowful about, and he radiates health, confidence and harmony wherever he goes.

Notice, the sad and sorrowful radiate sadness and sorrow.

The glad and joyous radiate joy and gladness.

One who believes in sickness and talks a great deal about sickness, sends forth diseased conditions.

One who believes in health as man's legitimate inheritance, will radiate health by his very presence.

The wise and original thinker radiates wisdom and originality.

The spiritually minded radiate life and vigor, strength and vitality.

It is only the spiritually minded who deal with principles and understand realities.

There is a natural and continual conflict between the materially educated and the spiritually minded, until the materialist begins to perceive something higher than the earthy stones and bones he has dealt with as realities heretofore.

It is the natural man that deals solely with material things, and believes in material laws, and consults the flesh on all matters pertaining to the earth life; and "the natural man receiveth *not* the things of the spirit, for they are foolishness unto him, neither can he know them because they are spiritually discerned."

Now, spiritual discernment is simply an interior perception, or knowledge of how Principle works, independent of material aids.

The spiritually minded have the majestic and all-conquering power of omnipotent wisdom to guide them, and by trusting it they are sure to win in every conflict.

The spiritually minded do not depend upon the theories and false ideas of the materialist, but lean upon the eternal truth as it dawns upon their interior perceptions; and what we lean upon for health, strength and judgment, strikes out and carries an influence to those with whom we associate, or in any way come in contact with.

We radiate health and confidence when we live in the absolute certainty that God is our health; and in the knowledge that there is no other source of health, and that we can appropriate all we need, and the supply never grows less. Acknowledge it continually, and your "light shall break forth as the morning (to shine upon all), and your health shall spring forth speedily."

Don't forget that whatever you think or believe carries an influence to others that *must* accord with the character of your thoughts and beliefs, whether audibly expressed or not.

When we are filled with the conviction that only the good is true and powerful, our very presence comforts and soothes the restless, fever-tossed patient, who has never before known anything better or higher than some nauseating drug to cool his fever.

He may not know from whence comes the sweet, soothing influence, and he wonders how he came to feel such peace, and such confidence that he is going to *pull through*, as he calls it; and this impression for good will not leave him; he will feel a prompting daily to seek a knowledge of this comforting influence, whatever it may be, and sooner or later the Christ will begin to be consciously acknowledged by him.

In this way you let your light shine, and Truth (Christ) is glorified in the result.

Even when the principles of science are only accepted *intellectually*, the influence radiated from such is better, higher and more up-lifting, than from those who grovel in material beliefs and ideas.

Many a case of healing has been accomplished by those who only receive the truth intellectually, but such are not fully anchored in the knowledge of spiritual supremacy, and are liable to be shaken from their foundation, because their foundation is only in the human intellect.

Their reasoning has not yet reached the point of conscious illumination by the spirit of truth.

Their faith is based upon what seems true from logical reasoning, and from what others have proved true, and they are on the right road to full understanding; but so long as it is not based upon actual knowledge by the interior perception they are liable to be shaken.

What we know by spiritual perception cannot be taken from us.

Those who accomplish healing by the intellectual perception only, are very apt to think they have a full understanding, because to them the human intellect is the highest; and until they seek the deeper spiritual certainty of truth in all its working power they will find themselves subject to all the ills and discords they formerly had, after the first enthusiasm cools.

It is the steadfast loyalty to Principle, and the constant acknowledgment of the supremacy of Spirit that closes the door to every discord, which practice soon brings the interior perception.

Paul said, "I would that thou affirm constantly, that they which have believed in God (in the good) might be careful to *maintain* good works."

You do not maintain good works when you allow mortality's claims to creep in after you have once turned them out by denial.

When you allow the old pains and discords to return, you are tempted to think that *after all* this science does not do for you what you had expected of it; you are apt to blame the science and forget to examine your own part in the matter.

If you are loyal to science, science will take care of you; but if you begin to relate in detail all the pains and aches that have returned, and describe all the bad symptoms you notice, as you did before knowing anything of the principles of science, you need not wonder if they stay by you in appearance, for recognition is all they ask.

You fellowship with error when you recognize it, and thus contradict the statements of science and leave the field to mortal error.

When you have grown to a full realization of the power of words you will not indulge in such complaints, for, "By thy words thou art justified, and by thy words thou art condemned."

The words of truth when spoken or thought with understanding and trust, will surely bear good fruit; but there must be an acknowledgment of the supremacy of Spirit.

The very knowledge of truth brings peace, because it is acknowledgment as well; and all suffering indicates that knowledge of truth is lacking.

You believe that God made all that really exists, and that He made all things good? Yes; then in reality there is no pain, sorrow or discord, and what seems so is mortal mind's delusion.

Never take the evidence of the senses unless they report according to righteous reason.

Your reason tells you that God never made pain, sorrow or discord, because all that He made is good—like Himself.

What could be more absurd than to suppose pain, sorrow or discord, could proceed from Life, Truth and Love?

It is not a reasonable supposition, therefore it is a delusion of mortal mind to even believe in them as realities.

As the drunken inebriate persists in his beastly appetite for strong drink until it culminates in *mania potu*, in which the snakes and toads and other reptiles are as real to him in his delirium as anything ever was in his lucid moments, he finds upon regaining his reason that all those horrid reptiles were only phantoms of his imagination, and never had any real existence.

Very similar is the experience of the suffering invalid who comes into the full light of this blessed truth.

When he comes to himself, as it were, he finds he had no disease at all, and what seemed so was the penalty for his mistake in believing in evil.

The picture of his error on his body may not be obliterated at the very moment he comes to himself, but with the change from error to truth, it will be manifest upon his body in due time.

We are to take no account of time at all. It is for us to hold firmly to the true word, and leave the result to the law (the Lord).

The time of its manifestation depends very largely upon our faithful adherence to Principle, regardless of what seems.

Never allow yourself to think it is not for you to receive this great blessing.

So many do this, and thus push away the very thing they so much desire.

It is like hanging up a thick curtain between you and the light, and then complaining of the darkness, saying the light is not for you.

Whatever we desire that is good is *God-prompted*. A desire that is good cannot be prompted by evil; and Jesus said, "*What things so-ever* ye desire when ye pray, *believe* that ye receive them, and ye shall have them."

The desire is of itself a promise according to the words of Jesus, but the condition of the promise is that you believe, or trust.

A very common mistake is made by wrongly interpreting our desires.

The man who indulges in stimulants supposes

that strong drink will satisfy his desires. He is mistaken in his desire, and he will often go on in his mistaken way of trying to satisfy a desire, until he sinks into utter ruin physically, morally and financially (seemingly), before he awakes to the fact that it is not strong drink that he wants at all.

When he does arouse himself to see his error, when he comes to himself, as it were, he sees that what he wanted was something that would satisfy his higher nature; he finds he was hungering and thirsting for righteousness (the right way), and when he begins in earnest to seek the right way it *does* satisfy his higher nature, and through the higher law he finds his physical body no longer requires a stimulant; he is happier without it, and better satisfied with himself altogether, and wonders how he ever could have so degraded himself.

The restless desire for something that will satisfy is so often left to the carnal nature to decide, that we are led into strange and devious ways in the search, never feeling certain whether we are seeking wisely or not; uncertainty makes us afraid, and the fear brings confusion.

Fear always shows forth in what we do not want; never in what we like.

Job said, "The thing I feared has come upon me."

All undesirable conditions, mental, physical or otherwise, are evidence that you believe in, and fear a law or power other than the good; thus we are constantly betraying our ignorance of truth, or our false beliefs, by our bodily and mental conditions.

To those who know the law the cause for disease and discord is often like an open book, even when the patient is wholly ignorant of it, but will attribute all such conditions to some material cause, bad air, impure water, malaria, over work, over heating, etc., none of which could so affect him if he understood his divine birthright, which teaches him the allness of good, wisdom to know the right, and nothing to fear.

Without this knowledge we grope in ignorance, and are misled in our desires, while knowing truth enables us to interpret our desires and thus reject the claims and suggestions of the carnal nature.

In this transition from ignorance to knowledge we go from a helpless, useless, wretched state of mind, to conscious power to speak peace to troubled hearts, and command health-giving thoughts, which are the working powers of mind; and the good we accomplish is the effect of conscious thinking upon unconscious conditions; by which we mean that thoughts build and control the unconscious body.

Our conscious thoughts are making continual changes in our bodily conditions.

As before stated, the story of the creation symbolizes the conscious mind of man.

Waters signifies the mind that thinks consciously and actively; that varies and changes like the waves of the sea; now animated—now placid and still—and again so turbid and angry as to simulate passion.

The dry land symbolizes the settled convictions of the mind; the fixed ways of thinking, the result of education and prejudice, that make the character fixed, and which characteristics externalize or picture forth upon the physical body and its organs, and are in science denominated unconscious mind.

Notice the distinction:

The conscious mind is that which acts upon the blood and secretions *immediately;* changing the quality and tone of the blood with every changing emotion or thought, thereby producing a corresponding change in the body and all its organs; therefore the body with its organs is the unconscious expression of past conscious thinking, and is called "*unconscious mind.*"

As it is the conscious thinking and believing that regulates the character of the blood, and operates with instant effect upon the functions and secretions, we must know that the conscious mind is responsible for all bodily changes.

This may be proved by any observing person in daily experience.

Every one knows that violent anger leaves one depressed and unhappy; which is only a beginning of the bad effects of anger. It is also well known that fear is very destructive to harmony of body.

To indulge in hateful sarcasm changes the character of the blood. Moment by moment the change goes on, till the quality of the blood produces a corresponding change in all the organs of the body.

To indulge in scorn and criticism and contemptuous sneers, no matter how much occasion you may think you have for such contempt, you not only augment the trait you so despise, but you yourself will take on a tinge of the same character, besides destroying the richness and sweetness of your own blood.

Your blood takes on an acid, watery condition, the result of your unwholesome state of mind, and the more you harbor the scorn and contempt the more thoroughly will that state of mind be photographed upon your unconscious body, which is like the sensitive plate in the camera, and reflects the exact state of mind you hold.

It is said that Emanuel Swedenborg in his moments of inspiration could see the change produced upon the physical organs of men by their thoughts.

He said that the changing, conscious thoughts change the action and character of the lungs, the heart, the stomach, the liver and kidneys, with lightning-like rapidity; just as the pictures on the screen change with the movements of the slide in the magic lantern; and our reason tells us that thoughts of love, and goodness, and truth, and charity could only produce harmony, because the law of the universe is harmony; and love, goodness, truth and charity are divine attributes which can only produce harmony.

The warm, loving thought of sympathy and good will and genuine charity toward a friend or neighbor, or even a foe, acts just as quickly; and such thoughts of love and kindness often work a sudden transformation, and the watery acids in the blood are turned to richness and sweetness, that show forth not only in bodily health, but in improved mental powers, purer motives and better character.

It is character that makes the man, and character that builds the body.

We want to look upon the physical body as simply the expression of mind, and nothing more.

To educate the mind in this philosophy opens our eyes to read character, and enables us to see all people in their true light.

Nothing will seem to us as it has in the past. Even our dearest friends, though we may have loved them very dearly, they have not been to us all they might have been, because we have always believed in the possibility of sickness and death, and of separation. In the realm of reality we see and know people as they really are, and there is no fear concerning them, and no belief in possible loss.

Instead of the hard, cold fear of death, the certainty of eternal life springs up, and all the former ways that worried and fretted us into sadness and despair, now turn blessed faces to cheer and comfort us; the reward for overcoming.

We overcome the fear of evil by learning the unreality of it. We overcome the fear of accident or misfortune by knowing we are folded round in safety from all evil. We overcome the fear of poverty by knowing that God's bounty is unlimited, and we are His children and can have all we claim in righteousness. We overcome the fear of death by knowing that in God is eternal life, that we are one with God, and heirs to eternal life.

What more can we ask than to be assured of freedom from all evil, protection from all harm, provided with all bounty, and eternal life as the crowning gift?

All this is ours without the asking; we only have to acknowledge it as already provided, and live consistent with the law that we set into action by our acknowledgment and trust.

We set the law to work just as soon as we silence the false claims of mortal mind. What we speak of in Science as mortal mind is that which yields to influences whether true or false. Its yielding character proves it mortal. It is that which takes what is false for truth as readily as that which is true, until it is trained to know truth and reject the false.

It is simply a reflection of the human intellect, and the farther it goes from truth the more distorted and unlike the substance it reflects.

It presumes to be mind, just as the counterfeit dollar presumes to pass for a genuine dollar but just as soon as it is known to be counterfeit it is worthless.

As soon as we know that the mortal mind (human judgment) is not reliable in its supposed knowledge of things, we begin to look to a higher source of knowledge, which is reliable.

This is the puzzling part of the great problem of life, apparently.

To be convinced without a single lingering

doubt that the mortal mind is only mortal; that it is but the imperfect shadow of the real, and wholly unreliable, is to find ourselves one with the mind that is God.

When we know the real we lose sight of the unreal sense world; that is, the reports of the mortal mind and the appearances of materiality are understood as nothingness.

"Old things have passed away, and behold, all things have become new"; which means when we are born into the understanding of things as they really are, all things are so changed to us that we see only the good.

We realize the nothingness of all materiality. As mortal mind is not mind at all in reality, so is the flesh man not *man* at all in reality.

The Adam man is nowhere referred to as the real creation of God that he pronounced good and perfect, and to whom he gave dominion.

He never gave dominion to the Adam man; Adam was the man of flesh, and the word traced back to its origin means error; and when the race began to look upon the flesh as the real man, the belief of sin and death came into the world, and man lost his dominion by falsely believing in the reality of the flesh.

All are familiar with the scriptural statement, " In Adam all die (which means in *error* all die), but in Christ (truth) all are made alive," and the law of sin and death is annulled by accepting truth.

We have to know and realize that the fleshly man is but the shadow, and so declare it, before we can prove it true; and to prove it we must reach the point of a positive statement, and fearlessly declare against all negation, and against all of mortality's claims regarding the flesh.

This is the very point in the teachings of Jesus where many of his acknowledged disciples "went away and walked no more with him."

He said, "The flesh profiteth nothing; it is the spirit that quickeneth," and they said, "This is a hard saying; who can hear it?" and they would have none of it. They went away and joined his enemies, and some of them afterward helped to crucify him.

They also said of Paul that he was a teacher of strange doctrines, a stirrer up of seditions, a pestilent fellow deceiving the people, while he was trying to make them understand the truth that would save them from all misery and wretchedness.

He wanted them to realize what the real, true self is; he wanted them to listen to the silent law that speaks within every man, woman and child that lives; that true school master we have heard so much about, and learned so little of what it means.

We have always heard about the true school master, but no one has ever told us how to consult it.

All the old philosophers and teachers and wise men of all ages, have recognized the importance of knowing the true self.

It was called by Pythagoras the "*salt* of men," and the "everlasting fountain of virtue."

Plutarch called it the "unerring guide."

Socrates called it the "Divine self." And John, the beloved disciple of Jesus, called it "the light that lighteth every man that cometh into the world."

We shall all find it to be the unerring counsellor if we consult it aright.

When we are willing to drop the claims of the mortal self and listen to this silent monitor, we "drop the old man with his deeds," as Paul expresses it, and "bring immortality to light."

It will prompt us to use the needful word in every case of healing. It guides us in our teaching of truth. It teaches us how to conduct our business affairs; how to live so that life is one unbroken succession of victories over evil. It is the only reliable guide, because it is the divine of us, and we are never without it; but as long as we look only to the negative, the nothing side, the shadow, we are not giving heed to the unerring guide at all.

It is faithful self-discipline that brings to the mind a realization of the true self.

The human intellect is always pushing its claims to the front, and we are easily deceived into thinking it really has a claim to supremacy, but according to Paul's experience, "The wisdom of men is foolishness with God," and when we find the divine self, which is always one with God, the human intellect of itself will seem foolishness to the divine self.

Of course we first have to accept or listen to this truth by the consent of the intellect or conscious mind, and thus we find that it is the conscious mind that needs the discipline, and has to be corrected of error.

It is *with* the conscious mind that we repeat over and over the words of truth in denial of mortality's claims, and we find them potent to erase the error.

Sometimes we are tempted to doubt the power of true words to accomplish the cleansing, even when we know the words are true; we do not doubt the truth of the words, but we doubt their potency; and we are very prone to doubt our own ability to use them with effect.

The evil condition as it seems, the discouraging circumstances, the sorrow and grief, all seem so real, and so impossible of removal by such a process, that the very thought seems presumption at first. And yet,—

Only the word of truth will make the desired change, and whether we accept it all at once, or come more gradually into an understanding of its principles, depends wholly upon ourselves.

It has been said that it takes the ordinary mind three years to train itself to really believe and see things as they are in truth, and cease to agree with the seeming, according to mortal sense.

The tenacity with which people cling to the old ways of thinking and believing is the principal obstacle to a quick realization of the true way.

Not many years ago we were taught that it took seven years for the human body to renew itself in all its parts; but now we know it only takes as many months when in perfect health.

Some French scientist, whose opinion seems to have been considered worthy of notice, has quite recently declared that the human body is wholly renewed in eleven months, which is the longest time *now* considered by any one of good judgment on the subject.

The old seven years theory has been discovered false and fallacious by investigations on a basis purely material, while with a knowledge of the mental forces we are much better able to judge of this process of renewal, because we know the functions and secretions act harmoniously or otherwise, according to the state of the mind and its understanding of law.

According to this statement the body is never more than eleven months old.

Then the question arises, why do we grow old in looks, in feelings, and in loss of vigor and vitality?

Simply because the ways of the world, the ideas and theories of men, all tend to such conditions. Men *believe* in time. Men *believe* in old age.

"As he thinketh in his heart, so is he," said Solomon.

If we believe in old age we grow old. If we believe in wear and tear we grow weary, and wear out in appearance.

It is all mortal belief in what is false.

It is all a lie. Nobody *can* grow old.

If we claim eternal life and acknowledge its source we shall renew our strength.

Did not the prophet Isaiah say in plain language, "They that wait upon the Lord shall renew their strength; they shall mount up with wings as eagles, they shall run and not be weary, they shall walk and not faint"?

To wait upon the Lord is to stand firm to true principles and trust the law to work for you.

All who plant their feet firmly on the rock truth, determined to stand by the scientific statements, report bodily changes in proportion to their trust in the law (Lord).

Improved health conditions, awakened intelligence, and sounder judgment, all come to the earnest-hearted student very quickly; and sooner or later the daily affairs of life begin to move in harmony with other improved conditions, and perfect peace of mind is established.

None of these happy changes ever come to us from depending upon external agencies for help, or upon drugs for health:

To know that the thoughts of the mind are the builders of the body, opens our eyes to the importance of training the mind in the ways of wisdom.

Our thoughts and beliefs are as much the creative word as when we speak them audibly, and true words are like seeds planted in fertile soil, which some day will bring forth good things to match the true thought or word.

> "Think truly, and thy thoughts
> Will the world's famine feed;
> Speak truly, and each word of thine
> Will be a fruitful seed;
> Live truly, and thy life will be
> A great and noble creed."

DYSPEPSIA CURED.

A lady who had suffered with chronic dyspepsia for many years, who thought she dared not eat meat, dared not eat vegetables, dared not eat hot cakes or warm bread, dared not drink coffee, and her tea must be very weak; in fact nothing could be suggested that she dared to eat; even oat meal with very thin milk gave her great pain, and she ate it with fear and trembling till she attended these lessons.

She commenced by saying this was her last hope. In less than a week she could eat whatever she liked without any disturbance or pain, and better still without fear of any further trouble.

She began to heal others before her first course of lessons was finished, and has been a very successful practitioner for more than three years, doing wonderful healing, and is also prospered as never before.

LESSON VI.

"With all thy getting, get understanding."

AS students of the *Science of Mind* it is well to know at the outset, that you are liable to meet with those who claim to understand science, and yet will seem to disagree with you on some points; which, if you are not watchful with your denials and affirmations, will confuse and depress you at first, or until your experience teaches you that nothing can hurt or discourage you.

There is not a righteous cause in existence that has not been more or less handicapped by poor representatives, and sometimes spurious advocates; all of which has nothing to do with Principle.

You have the infallible rule by which to judge of what is true and scientific. Whatever does not accord with the Statement of Being (which acknowledges but one power in the universe), must be rejected as false and misleading.

If any one tells you there is a power called

malicious, animal magnetism, or mesmerism, you want to deny it at once *with firmness*, lest you allow fear to get the upper hand.

There *is* no such power.

There are many Scientists of a certain class who have been led to believe in this seeming power, and they have made so much of it, and their attention has been given so largely to the fear of it, that they seem to be losing their power to heal; losing their peace of mind, and also their health, by it.

Such belief is a plain contradiction of the statements they set out with, and can only lead to confusion.

Whoever believes in any such power betrays a lack of understanding of the principles of science, besides showing very plainly that they lean upon some personality more than upon that Divine Principle which is the only Reality.

Pay no attention to what people say against or for teachers of the science.

If you want to be proficient in knowledge, *study the science instead of the scientists.*

Stand by the principles in all your ways, and your understanding will save you from confusion.

If you allow every criticism to move you there will be no peace for you.

Never in the history of the world has there

been a new and startling discovery of principles, or an innovation that set aside the old ways, that did not meet with scorn, criticism, opposition and persecution; and the calumnies that have been heaped upon discoverers, as well as upon the advocates of mighty principles, have driven many to despair; and it was left for students of Science to discover a law by which calumny and persecution are made powerless to hurt any righteous cause. We render them powerless by understanding the righteous law.

If you notice very closely you will observe that those who misrepresent and scorn the new Science, sooner or later lose their standing and influence, and often sink into a state of inability to even conduct their business affairs successfully.

They turn the law against themselves unwittingly by their unrighteous persecution of a righteous cause; which they would not do if they understood the law.

The law works with the same accuracy when one who professes an understanding of the science criticises, defames or misrepresents another.

The law is no respecter of persons; and every professing Christian, whether a scientist or not, is in duty bound to further the cause of this practical Christianity instead of hampering it by persecution and calumny.

Of course the science is invulnerable, and cannot be hurt; and every weapon aimed at it by prejudice and ignorance, or by jealousy and malice, will act as the boomerang, and only strike the one who hurls it.

When Peter and John were tried before a council of Scribes and Pharisees for teaching this same doctrine, Gamaliel, who was held in high esteem, remonstrated against the proceedings. Jew as he was, he seemed to have a noble sense of justice in this case, worthy of emulation.

After reminding the council how every unrighteous scheme came to naught, he said: "Refrain from these men, and let them alone, for if this work be of men it will come to naught, but if it be of God *ye* cannot overthrow it."

What a wise conclusion!

Some day the world will see how useless it is to try to stay the spread of this majestic truth.

For eighteen centuries it has withstood all attempts to extinguish it, though sometimes its light has grown very dim (in appearance), and many have wondered why all the healing and comforting, and blessed ministrations of the gospel of Christ had vanished and left Christians without a Christ ministry.

Understanding the Principle, and standing by the principles for Principle's sake, the science will **take care of you.**

Your defense is in the law.

In studying science you study God. Science teaches us to be wise and God-like; and charity and love set the God-like powers to do great works

Power comes with understanding.

We do not have to read a great number of books in order to understand science.

We enter upon the study of science by the willing acceptance of its first principles, and when it dawns upon the interior perception it is as if we were entering into a new country.

Every student of science will receive that interior knowledge in his own way, and the stock of information already stored in the mind has much to do with helping or hindering his understanding.

The study of mind or metaphysical law tends to develop strong mental powers, even on the plane of the human intellect; while to study Spirit with the realization that Spirit is the only Reality, and Spirit and Mind are One, gives us the key to all power. Then we can say with Paul, "I can do all things through Christ which strengtheneth me."

Christ is the spirit of truth.

We grow to be like what we study most; and by studying the truth we become Christ-like in powers, and can do the same works Christ did.

To study Mind or Spirit as a healing principle, we become a healing force.

We develop the Christ-power within us, in the line of healing.

The mind that develops the healing force in greatest perfection will manifest the healing power in three different ways.

That is, there is a three-fold change wrought by the well trained healing mind.

Bodily health, moral rectitude, and awakened intelligence, must always be shown as signs of perfect healing.

The bodily health is generally the first sign sought for, and usually the first manifest; but the other changes come in due time, often as the result of study and practice of the divine principle of healing.

The moral change and intellectual awakening are not so quickly manifest in the patient as in the faithful student, while the healing is often accomplished very speedily by another mind.

Let it be understood that it is always the Christ within you that accomplishes the healing.

No one can doubt that the greatest powers of the Christ were shown by the good works He did, which were mostly works of healing.

"The secret law" is the law of healing and working miracles.

We read that he "took his disciples apart" when he taught them these powers, because it was not lawful for him to teach it openly.

When teaching the multitudes, he taught the same doctrine, but was obliged to teach *them* in parables, which even to this day are obscure in their meaning to many, especially to those who only read on the surface.

It is only within the past twenty-five or thirty years that this philosophy could have been taught openly, even here in this "so-called" enlightened land; and even now it is not uncommon to hear of people who fancy it ought to be suppressed; which, of course, is only because of their ignorance of its principles.

Such opposition will all die out sooner or later, as all error must.

Everything that opposes the healing mind, or the righteous endeavor to set the law of harmony into action by the powers of mind, can be met and mastered by that mind.

When you speak the word of truth you set the principle of truth into action, and the truth principle by its very nature heals, saves, makes free. It is the law.

Jesus means Saviour, the same as Joshua. Jesus was the Christ (Truth), and he saves by the Christ Principle. To heal and to save are synonymous terms.

When Jesus said, "Lo, I am with you alway," he was speaking of the divine of him, the Christ, which is the son of God. When speaking of himself as Jesus he called himself the "son of man."

All have the Christ within, and it works the works of God through us in proportion to our acknowledgment of its power and presence, and our loyalty to it, by the exclusion of error from the conscious mind by righteous reasoning.

It is often asked why the pious and devout for ages past have failed to accomplish such results by their devotion to the cause of Christ.

They have not recognized the Christ within them at all; neither have they been loyal to Principle, to the exclusion of error.

Preachers and teachers and philanthropists all over the civilized world have mixed a little truth with a *great deal* of error.

The pulpit has always given power and sway to another power beside the good.

The press have always done the same, and are still holding up this great power of evil and turning the world over into its clutches as if they hated to mention the good side of anything, or see any one loosen the coils of evil.

They gather up statistics of crime and records of horrors and scent out every unclean transaction that reflects an unwholesome influence, and then wonder at the awful depravity in the world, and deplore the weakness and inefficiency of religious methods and moral reforms to stay such evils.

Evil and the power of evil are held up and given such prominence that many really believe it to be greater than the power of good.

People are not aware that they invoke that which they name and give place to and believe in.

They give it working efficiency in seeming by recognition and acknowledgment. Discord is the result.

When we realize the majesty, and wisdom, and power, and absolute all-ness of the good, and so acknowledge it, we invoke that adorable Intelligence, we set it into action, and harmony is the result.

We invoke the majestic Principle of health when we name it as Divine, and trust its working power, and believe in its law.

These lessons treat of much that the natural man cannot understand.

They treat of spiritual principles, which are only clear to the interior perceptions; but in this way we are led to the "gateway of understanding." We "speak the mystic word that lets us in."

Some of the first statements of the science demand the rejection of the evidence of the senses when their reports are not in harmony with reason, and the natural man rebels against that demand, because *he* judges solely by the senses. He judges by the senses because he has not opened his mind to receive the deeper knowledge which deals with principles only.

"Whoso is spiritual hath all power, for Spirit worketh for him."

When we let the Spirit work for us (that is, when we trust Principle), the hard ways of life and human experience are utterly forgotten.

Pain and heart sorrows are swept away, and we forget we ever had them even in seeming.

Something comforts us with sweet assurance that all is right, and blessings unknown in former days seem showered upon us without the asking.

New understanding of the ways of life dawns upon us.

We have new perceptions of law. We even see how the writers of Scripture in their highest moments of inspiration could foresee how Divine law would work; and we see how they recognized only the Good as a working principle in the universe.

When we have caught but a slight perception

of the supremacy of Spirit, we see that those inspired writers knew evil as unreality and all matter as but the expression of something real.

The Psalmist David said, "Only with thine eyes shalt thou behold and see the reward of the wicked."

As much as to say, *It is only by sense evidence* that you behold and see the false conditions that mortal error (which he calls wickedness) produces. Spiritual perception takes no account of it; knows it not, because it is not real.

"He that shutteth his eyes from seeing evil, he shall dwell on high; his place of defense shall be the munitions of rocks, bread shall be given him, and his waters shall be sure." Evidently the prophets and inspired writers knew that spiritual law is the only law, and material phenomena are but shadows of the real.

Spiritual creation is the only creation, and the shadow is mortal mind's conception of it.

To mortal mind the material seems the only creation, because the finite or mortal mind "perceiveth not the things of the spirit," but looks upon the shadow as the real.

The conscious mind is mortal or carnal so long as it allows the evidence of the senses to decide for it, but when the conscious mind is willing to be guided by the interior perceptions, it casts off the carnal mortal nature, and is renewed in the image and likeness of God, and becomes one with the Divine Self.

When thus born into the understanding of truth the mortal puts on immortality, and as the physical is plastic to the thoughts and beliefs of the conscious mind, it very soon responds to the change and begins to take on a more perfect state of health, symmetry and happy expression very remarkable in many cases.

The change is often so wonderful that it seems like a new creation; and yet the perfection was there all the time, concealed by false ideas and mortal beliefs.

We do not *create*, but we do a similar work. By a knowledge of law, we speak the perfection that already exists, into visible manifestation; and in proportion as we train the conscious mind to know and understand this law, will the carnal nature lose control. In proportion as we consecrate our life to the work of destroying error and the belief in evil, will we be powerful in correcting the carnal nature in others.

In works of healing you are correcting mortal error exactly the same as if you were treating for immorality.

Mortal error shows forth in many ways besides. upon the body; sometimes in ill tempers, sometimes in immoral traits of character, sometimes in morbid fancies; and every patient who comes for healing, shows by his bodily condition that his life problem has all been wrought according to mortal error.

The conditions he complains of are the proof of his ignorance of the power of truth to set things right. In his ignorance he yields to the suggestions of the carnal nature, which is not subject to the law of the good, hence the confusion, the disease.

The whole human family live in an atmosphere of mortal beliefs in sickness, and mortal beliefs regarding causes, which beliefs tend continually to produce the very thing they believe in and fear.

If we are open and receptive to those false influences and beliefs, we shall probably suffer the consequence; but if we are fortified by a knowledge of the truth that saves, and makes free, we shall not succumb to any such prevailing physical troubles.

Without this knowledge and constant realization as a defense against mortal error, the sickness is liable to come.

Whoever catches the belief that health is the legitimate inheritance of every one, will refuse to be sick, no matter what prevails in the way of epidemics, contagions or whatever.

They appropriate health by the very character of their thoughts.

Those who believe in the epidemic and fear it will appropriate the sickness.

The belief in health as our rightful inheritance must be based on knowledge of divine law in mental action, else it is liable to be overthrown.

The conscious mind needs to know that the health is the showing forth of the true self, in order to make it unfailing.

The conscious mind must never admit that health can be destroyed.

Health is one of the imperishable attributes of God. *That is*, it belongs in the category of perfect divine Principle. Health is God; therefore it is indestructible; there is no such thing as *poor* health, *feeble* health, *miserable* health, etc. Health is health, and it cannot be qualified by any such adjectives; and when we fully realize the unchangeable, indestructible character of the actual self of us, the child of God, we begin to prove its perfection and excellence by making the physical show forth in visible signs of perfection and harmony.

To think and speak a great deal of spiritual perfection and harmony as your rightful inheritance, makes it show forth; you build as you think.

It is the business of the conscious mind to first know truth, then prove its knowledge true by making harmony manifest.

We let our light shine by making harmony manifest in our environments, as well as in bodily health.

We let our light shine when we speak health into manifestation for a patient.

We let our light shine when we teach others the way, and at the same time obey the command to preach the gospel, and heal the sick.

All who know this mighty truth can make it shine forth in *some* way, if only in proclaiming the law, by the silent rejection of all mortality's claims, and affirming the truth. Even children can be taught to make the good manifest by refusing to see evil.

In whatever way we use the law we increase our understanding of it, and we find new truths dawn upon us daily.

New and higher perceptions come as a reward for faithfully serving Truth.

You need to be very thorough and earnest with your self-discipline, and reject all falsity; deny all the claims of mortal mind, and all the claims of matter as a reality, and all the evils you have ever believed in, until every pain and sorrow, and every undesirable condition sinks out of sight, and you realize that "only the good is true."

Don't say you can't do it.

You *can* do it; every one can do it, but you can't do it by holding the thought that you can't. If you sit in the silence alone and force your conscious mind to drop all thoughts of a negative character, by which I mean the *not desirable*, and cease to think or speak of the changing, perishing character of the material world about you, and think and speak only of that which is true and deathless, everything will begin to take on the deathless perfection you have in mind.

Think and speak persistently of the divine of you, and the divineness of your inheritance.

Make the declaration over and over (mentally) that you are a child of Wisdom, a child of harmony, a child of perfection, and you will find wisdom, harmony and perfect conditions manifest in your life.

Remember that so much wisdom, harmony and perfection as you make manifest in your life, just so much of the divine of you is manifest.

Being a child of perfection in every sense you must realize the necessity of acknowledgment. "Acknowledge me in all thy ways and I will direct thy paths."

Jesus said, "Call no man upon earth your Father, for one is your Father, even God."

You see how Jesus in his teaching spoke continually of the *real*, actual of our being.

He never spoke of God as the father of the flesh man, and all his teachings tend to show the nothingness of all flesh, as well as of all evil, which is the offspring of our false beliefs regarding the flesh.

When we consider that the flesh man is only the outward expression of our thoughts and beliefs, we shall realize the importance of thinking and believing in harmony with divine law.

As we see the folly of believing in and fearing an evil power, the mist is cleared away, and all the rubbish of former ways of thinking goes with it. Then dawns upon us the beauty of knowing realities, and the certainty that we can prove them true.

We prove them by the wonderful power of the word.

"Without the word was not anything made that was made."

We "receive the spirit of adoption" by knowing the true nature of our inheritance, and declaring it.

Always speak to the true self of you in your self-discipline; not to the mortal at all, and when treating a friend or neighbor or patient whose mortal ways need correcting, call mentally to the real self of him and this will set him right.

It is not the true self of him that does the wrong.

To call him by name (mentally) and tell him of his spiritual birthright to perfection and goodness, will set his whole conscious nature into harmony with his divine nature.

You lift the mortal nature out of its sordidness and sensuality by calling the true self into manifestation, and the mortal begins to put on immortality, or is swallowed up in immortality.

This is the kind of service that brings us into union with Christ. It gives us the mind that was in Christ. By understanding the spirit of His teaching, and keeping his words till we are alive with their meaning, we are letting the same eternal mind that He called the Father speak through us.

This is the only true atonement, or at-one-ment, which has always been misunderstood.

We have always been taught that the blood of Christ atoned for our sins, the literal blood; but never has it been explained to the satisfaction of any rational mind by the usual view of the vicarious atonement.

No one ever taught us that the blood was only a symbol of the true word, and that the word was Life, Spirit.

Jesus said, "The words that I speak unto you are spirit, and they are life."

The blood of Christ means the word of truth, and He tells us to drink of it; that is, to take it into our inmost understanding, as we would drink of refreshing water when thirsty; accept it, and abide in it, which makes us *one* with it.

It makes us one with eternal life, one with absolute truth; the only rational at-one-ment.

This may all seem very metaphysical to one who has not reasoned on this line, as it all relates to mind, and the various states of mind, which is the only way to understand the physical.

When we think and talk of physical states and conditions we are thinking and talking about mere negation; and from the fact that we necessarily grow to be like what we study, think about and believe in, you can readily understand how dull and negative we grow by believing in and calculating for the physical as the real.

This dull negative state hides our conception and understanding of what is true; it is the "natural man that perceiveth not the things of the spirit, neither can he know them, because they are spiritually discerned."

There can be no spiritual discernment where the conscious mind clings to the negative.

Spiritual discernment is simply understanding of truth.

When we have trained the mind into a persistent determination to ignore the false and only accept what accords with divine law, we are rewarded with new light in proportion to our thorough rejection of the false, and hearty acceptance of the true.

This new light is spiritual discernment. It is conscious understanding. We *know* whereof we speak.

When we say that as Spirit we are children of the Good, our reason pushes us to say, that as flesh we are children of evil (negative—not good).

Spirit is the eternal verity; flesh is only the picture—the deception—prone to error. It is both deceiver and deceived.

It is always dying because the mind that controls it is carnal. "To be carnally minded is death."

Notice the distinction: "To be spiritually minded is life and peace." It is wisdom to be spiritually minded because the life and peace are mirrored in our earth lives as well. We are not afraid of death nor anything that leads to death.

"Ye are of your Father, the devil," was said of the Adam nature, the error nature, not of the real man at all. It is a commonly accepted statement of Orthodoxy that, "In Adam all die"; which is equivalent to saying that error leads to death. The Adam nature is the carnal nature. To be carnally minded is death.

Now, "In Christ all are made alive"; which is the same as saying: In truth is life, health and peace; for it is truth that makes us free from one evil as much as another.

The term, "*In Christ*," means to be in conscious understanding of Truth as Jesus taught it, and to live consistent with it; or in a state of oneness with the spirit of Christ; to have a constant realization of what is true and deathless, which is the kingdom of heaven, brought into manifest reality here and now.

If we look only at what the eyes of flesh tell us, we see the exact opposite of the kingdom of heaven. We dwell in the carnal nature, and see only what leads to death.

Now we cannot know or understand the law of the shadow, till we know that of the substance which casts the shadow. We cannot know what the flesh is until we understand the mind.

Why are we commanded to "seek *first* the kingdom of God and His righteousness"? Then we have the promise that all other desirable things will be added unto us.

In seeking the kingdom of God, by which is meant the Real kingdom of Good, which is only revealed to us by right thinking, we get all the good we can wish for or desire.

We are not seeking the kingdom of God and His righteousness when we follow shadows, nor when we complain of our burdens, nor when we fear evil, for the kingdom of God is found by acknowledgment.

When we begin to declare with confidence that Spirit is the only substance, and all that *is*, is good, everything begins to show forth signs of the truth we have spoken; we find the good, and only the good, in everything we touch.

Health takes the place of sickness, happiness takes the place of misery, harmony takes the place of discord and poverty gives place to plenty.

When we ignore the false and unreal, and turn to the Substance, all things will turn blessed faces to us, and we can truly say the kingdom of heaven is at hand.

Truly, "Old things have passed away, and behold all things have become new."

We enter this kingdom whenever we obtain an understanding of gospel truth as Jesus taught it.

He taught us to pray for this kingdom to come on the earth as it is in heaven; and yet among all the thousands who offer that prayer daily, scarcely one is willing to even admit the possibility of ever bringing it to pass; and the few who verily believe and understand how it may be brought to pass are looked upon as visionary enthusiasts, and often called blasphemers, and every obstacle is placed in the way to prevent them from proving their way of understanding correct.

The Saviour taught that the kingdom of heaven is not a place or location, and said, "Neither shall they say lo here, or lo there, for behold, the kingdom of God is within you."

The kingdom of heaven is conclusively a state of the mind, and if the conscious mind receives the truth in all its fullness while in the earth life then is when the kingdom of heaven is come upon the earth.

By the practice of Science we endeavor to bring it to pass exactly in accordance with the teachings of the Master, by destroying the works of the devil, which can never be accomplished by any other plan than by a knowledge of truth as the Master taught it.

Now, to understand the unity of the mind of man with the mind that is God, is knowledge more profound than all the wisdom of the schools. It lifts us out of bondage. It opens prison doors. It feeds the hungry. It heals the sick. It comforts the sorrowing. It is the truth that makes free. It is the knowledge that profiteth with joy forever more.

By knowing this we know all things.

Knowledge is power because knowledge is of God.

"Wisdom is with him that hath understanding, and they that understand shall be wise and do exploits."

It is found by faithfully holding and keeping the true word, and it is made potent by the acknowledgment of its source and divine origin.

"With all thy getting get understanding."

RHEUMATISM CURED.

A young lady who was greatly afflicted with rheumatism, with joints swollen and warped out of all natural proportions, going on crutches, was induced to have treatment and at the same time attend a course of lessons.

Treatments were given each day for a week, after which she acknowledged herself cured, and was confident that with the knowledge she had gained by the lessons she should never be troubled again with rheumatism.

Her father and brother were also victims of the same delusion, and although they ridiculed the idea at first, she persevered with both until they acknowledged the healing.

Whoever studies these lessons with care and follows the teaching can do the same.

HEALED BY THESE LESSONS.

St. Louis, Mo., July 18, '91.

Dear Mrs. Yarnall:—I feel truly glad to hear that you are having your lessons published in book form. To me they were priceless.

You have the rare gift of logically translating the spiritual into the practical. In them I found no metaphysical abstractions; the sweet, plain truth made as clear and strong in its ready application to every day life, as it is enlightning to the spiritual senses.

Place me on your subscription list, and remember me as yours with gratitude and love.　　Mrs. Vintie McDonald,
1017 Chestnut st., St. Louis, Mo.

By putting in practice the beautiful principles you taught me with such forcible clearness, I have overcome all tendency to the many physical ills I formerly suffered, chief among which were the most terrible headaches, which had baffled all previous attempts to relieve them; besides opening the way to peace of mind in which I find perfect immunity from anxious care.

St. Louis, Mo.　　E. C. Gilmore.

Your teaching of the principles of the Christ Science has not only shown me the way out of physical suffering, but opened my understanding and enabled me to realize my true self as the child of God. The Bible is no longer a sealed book. I find my mental capacities enlarged, and the old narrow conception of Divine law has given place to a positive knowledge that it is God's will that we should be well and happy.　　Mrs. F. Johnson.

St. Louis, Mo.

Every lesson came to me as a revelation, permeating my entire being. I was hungering for more light on the science of mind; hungering also for health and strength physically, being still a sufferer from old chronic troubles that had rendered my life a burden for years.

As I listened to your lessons the beauty and power of knowing Divine realities dawned upon me with such vivid realization that I soon found my health and comfort restored.

I was led step by step out of the labyrinths of error into the light of freedom, and I can truly say I am sound and well, and that my path grows brighter and brighter in the light of the truth as you taught me.

You have the heartfelt gratitude of myself and wife for the help you have given in opening to us the door to knowledge and wisdom. Ever thine in truth. DR. U. M. HUMBLE.

I was cured of pleurisy and serious lesion of the lungs, and what was supposed to be hereditary consumption, under your teaching, and for four years I have not taken a dose of any medicine, except words of truth. LOUISE NELSON.

Lincoln, Neb.

From girlhood I had been a victim to ill health and violent sick headaches, which occurred once a week, lasting from 24 to 36 hours.

All schools of medicine, as well as mineral waters and changes of climate, had utterly failed to give relief.

Three years ago my husband and myself learned, by attending a course of lessons with you, that if we governed our lives by the teachings of Jesus, we have the power to overcome all inharmony. By your teachings we learned how to overcome error. Since then I have never had a sick headache. I regard my cure as one of the signs that Jesus said should follow them that believe.

Gratefully your friend and pupil,

Dallas, Tex., July, 1891. MRS. W. H. JOHNSON.

I was healed of a very distressing stomach trouble, besides other less serious maladies, by attending your lessons. Was perfectly well before I completed my first course of lessons, and since then have demonstrated the truths of Divine Science by healing many of the physical and mental inharmonies of people who came to me for help. MRS. E. W. MORGAN.

Lincoln, Neb.

By your teaching alone I was lifted from the depths of despair, mentally and physically. Being consumptive, suffering with bronchitis, catarrh and asthma, I was made well.

At the second lesson my sprained foot, which was swollen out of all shape, was healed perfectly well; since which time I have neither taken nor given a single dose of material medicine in my family, and all fear of sickness has vanished.

Sherman, Texas. MRS. M. L. HUNTER.

After years of suffering with liver and kidney troubles, and finding all medicines, climates and mineral waters of no avail, in my despair I seemed to be led to Mrs. Yarnall. I took both lessons and treatments, and the second day during the lesson and treatment I felt that I was healed.

It was the happiest day of my life, and I say, God bless the workers in the healing science *everywhere*. A. M.

I was for thirty years afflicted with hernia in its most serious form, never daring to stand on my feet a moment without my truss securely adjusted.

I attended a course of lessons with Mrs. Yarnall, during which time I laid aside my truss, and for four years have been perfectly free from the former trouble. J. C. H.

After many years of suffering, and five years a confirmed invalid, during which time many able physicians had pronounced my case utterly hopeless, I was cured, sound and well, in three days, by listening to your lessons (beginning with no confidence whatever), and for three years have been blessed in the work of healing others. MARY ORR.

Del Norte, Col.

I am rejoiced to be able to testify that by your lessons alone, without any treatment except the discipline you taught us, I was changed in one short month from a nervous, miserable invalid to a sound, well woman, and for three years and over I have rejoiced in perfect health, strength and endurance beyond all expectation; but the physical change sinks into insignificance compared with the mental and spiritual. I never before knew what the peace that passeth understanding meant. M. A. LEAKE.

Dallas, Texas.

ST. LOUIS, MO., June 23, 1891.

My Dear Mrs. Yarnall:—I have found potency, power and truth in the words of your teaching. They voice the true sentiment of life, peace, health and love. The more I ponder on the work of the words you have spoken to me, the more I feel like "a strong man to run a race." Your lectures have pointed out to me a new way, and I feel more clearly through your teaching the light of the life that never goes out. Respectfully,

C. J. GRIFFITH.

I esteem it a privilege to testify to the healing and harmonizing effects of your lessons upon all who hear them.

They promote harmony in every department of life; they remove all fear of sickness, and heal the heartaches as nothing else can.

They open a new Heaven and a new Earth, and therefore bless mankind by establishing the knowledge of truth that makes us free. W. I. SMITH.

St. Louis, Mo.

PART II.

LESSON VII.

"He sent his word and healed them."

ON first taking up the study of the healing Science, the student often experiences a feeling of discouragement and doubt of his or her ability to grasp the truth in such fullness as to be able to heal the sick by it.

There seems to be so much to remember, and there is such a complete turning about from old ways and old beliefs, that have formerly been so firmly relied upon, that the change seems like a leap in the dark. Then we remember that the change from the old false ways is what we are seeking, and we know that no good can come from the new way while we hold to the old.

There can be no dividing of honors.

The old ways which brought you only pain and discord are false, and are entitled to *no honors*.

If the new way brings you peace and harmony it is true, and is entitled to all honor.

Truth is a jealous God, and will not divide honors with error.

Divine Science could not be a true science if it could be made to deviate from exactness.

You would consider the science of mathematics very imperfect and unreliable if it would admit of now and then a little deviation from the true calculation to accommodate the whim of some student of mathematics.

Science is Science only when it is exact, and Divine Science is no exception, but is rather the Science of all sciences; and all failures to obtain correct results by the science are due to lack of understanding of Divine law, just as all failures to get true answers to your mathematical problems are due to your lack of understanding of the principles of mathematics.

There is nothing wrong with the science in either case.

The trouble is all in the various whims of the mortal mind that thinks it dare not launch out beyond the reach of old errors, although the old errors have yielded only discord and discomfort.

It is the turning away from old time-honored fallacies that people are afraid of, and yet the turning away is what does them good.

They will say they are afraid to do without the doctor in sickness for fear something might happen.

Something *does* happen very often when they have the doctor, and even when they have three or four of them.

One old lady said nothing could induce her to do without her doctor in sickness. He had stood by her faithfully for twenty years, and she had buried nine children who all died under his care, and now that her husband was about to die she thought it would be very ungrateful to discard his services; he was always such a comfort at the funeral.

Another old lady said she never allowed herself to be without calomel and jalap in the house; they acted so powerfully in sickness.

Such people are honest and sincere, and never dream how ludicrous their ideas seem to the advanced thinker.

The ways of mortal mind are the inventions of the carnal nature, which is always opposed to the good, and it is better to turn your back firmly upon the false way right in the beginning.

If you have been a sufferer from some chronic malady, and thought you must make a laboratory of your stomach, don't imagine that you must break off *gradually* from your eighteen doses daily; no; "Throw all physic to the dogs" at once.

If it had ever done you any good you would have found it out ere this; and if it does *no* good, the sooner you break off the better.

Let the Principle that created you heal you.

By trusting it, you set it to work, and you cannot trust it while you cling to old idols.

The shortest way to success is the straight and narrow way.

Put aside all fear of being misled.

Don't be persuaded by any one to think it a dangerous doctrine that does not teach belief in an angry God, a burning hell and a personal devil.

Science has proved it to be dangerous to *believe* such wicked absurdities.

Science proves that what we believe in, and think about, is shadowed forth in our life.

If we believe in an angry God, we shall be continually haunted by fear of offending Him.

If we believe in a burning hell, our lives will be tortured by miseries that constitute hell; and if we believe in an individual personal devil—"going about like a roaring lion, seeking whom he may devour"—we shall live in perpetual dread.

All things go to prove that heaven and hell are states of mind.

By the devil that Jesus likened to a roaring lion, etc., is evidently meant the evil propensities of the human heart, which are constantly urging us to let the carnal selfish nature have control. Those propensities devour us in seeming.

They *consume* us, mortally speaking.

Did not the Psalmist David say, "The pains of hell gat hold upon me"? which in his case was as much the result of carnal foolishness as with any one else.

David had the wisdom to repent and turn from carnal foolishness, and his beautiful songs of praise are the outpourings of a grateful soul to the Lord, who "delivered him from his distresses."

The pains of hell which David suffered were evidently distress of mind.

Did we ever get any comfort or heavenly delight in the thought of an angry God?

Did it ever give us comfort or peace to believe in a burning hell that the angry God had prepared for his disobedient children?

Did we ever get comfort or satisfaction in the belief that God created us totally wicked and depraved, with a strong tendency to disobedience, and no knowledge of how to remedy the tendency? No! No! No! to all such questions.

Then let us abandon all beliefs that do not bring harmony into our lives.

If we would have health of body we must begin with harmony of mind, and we must know that false ways and false ideas never bring harmony.

Solomon said: "There is a way that seemeth right unto a man, but the end thereof are the ways of death."

Solomon knew that the ways of mortal error were disappointing and misleading.

Paul expressed the same sentiment when he said: "To be carnally minded is death."

Carnal ways and sordid desires have always *seemed* to be the way to gain satisfaction, but they have always found death at the end.

Now the ways of science tend continually to life.

Jesus said: "I come that ye might have life, and that ye might have it more *abundantly*." That is, to let the life-giving principle reign supreme.

There is a life-giving quality in the teachings of science that no other Christian teachings have ever had, and the vital principle makes its impression in such unmistakable ways that no faithful student can doubt or forget the principles.

With the thorough discipline we advise, the truth sinks deeper and deeper till you thoroughly understand and are at one with it.

The eager anxiety to master the whole philosophy at once is very natural and common, but is often a hindrance.

It betrays the fact that you are looking too eagerly for what the intellect approves.

You are not yet aware that you must "leap the bounds of the human intellect."

To "wait patiently on the Lord (the law), you enter a realm of thought and understanding so far above and beyond the comprehension of mere sense perception (which is all the intellect depends upon), that you are astonished at the unreliability of the human intellect when *un*illumined by spiritual perception.

When doubts arise and you feel enveloped in mental darkness, as you are liable to at first, you have the remedy always at hand.

Deny the darkness and doubt with vigor and assurance till it disappears.

Your self-training will always set you right if you use it with trust.

As long as you talk or think doubtfully of your understandiug or ability, the darkness and doubt will grow deeper.

If you talk and think about not knowing, you fellowship with ignorance and you grow more and more negative until you become a complete picture of negation and doubt, which is a helpless condition.

Never admit your doubts, either by thought or word, but constantly affirm wisdom as your divine inheritance; hold patiently to affirmations of wisdom and strength and harmony, and your doubts have vanished before you know it. Your confidence is secured.

Never admit the negative, the not good, the *uncertain*, in any case ; but boldly hold to the positive good, the definite and *certain*, for, "By thy words thou art justified, and by thy words thou art condemned."

Now, as before stated, the conscious mind which does the thinking, is responsible for all bodily conditions, all circumstances and environments; therefore, according to the character of our thoughts and beliefs in the past, so do our bodies, our circumstances and environments show forth now; and according as we think and believe *now* will we produce corresponding conditions in the future.

Put aside every thought that would foster a belief in disease. For instance, the belief in physical causation is wonderfully prolific of sickness.

Notice the result of the ages of study of physics.

Those who devote themselves to the study of physics, go on year after year seeking for causes for this, that and the other, with no perceptible benefit to the world.

It is just dawning upon the minds of those who notice, that diseases (according to mortal sense) are actually propagated by the investigations and conclusions of men who devote their time to such study.

Medical records are furnishing proofs of this statement (unintentionally) every year. The great and famous experts in special diseases have, in some cases, studied and thought in the one line of investigation till their own bodies have taken on the very diseases they were seeking causes for.

Quite recently a healthy, robust physician of New York, who had spent months and years on the study of insanity and its causes, prepared a most able treatise on the subject, which he read before a medical society. He went home from the meeting as insane as the cases he had described, and killed his wife and children and himself as a result of his study of dementia.

He believed in insanity, and his belief was intensified by the constant study of the theme.

In the study of causation on a physical plane, no one ever dreams of mental causes.

Their microscopic investigations often reveal the presence of organic life in the air we breathe, and in the water we drink; and upon further investigation they find the same organic life in the patient who suffers an attack of the prevailing epidemic, and their conclusions are all based upon those investigations.

There has been no attempt on the part of physicians to analyze or study the mental conditions that act upon the functions, and produce such marvelous changes.

How, according to physical causation, do they account for the fact that one of a family will be stricken with a fever, while none of the others take it, although all have lived in the same atmosphere and drank of the same water?

All answers to such questions are weak and unsatisfactory, which goes to prove how unreliable material science is, and that much of the so-called science of pathology is guess-work.

Many of the most eminent physicians of the age have candidly admitted that "the most they *know* is that they know nothing."

As believers in Divine law we know that mortal mind is the cause of all discord.

The work of mortal mind is to imitate the ways and creations of Immortal Mind, and the deceptive character of its imitations makes them seem like real creations to those who only know what the senses tell them.

We know that mortal mind creates what *seems*, as delirium tremens creates snakes and toads.

Mortal mind would have no knowledge of organic life in the air and water, if no one went in search for such things with his microscope.

Have they removed the trouble by investigation or augmented it by increasing the fears?

All such laws as mortal mind invents can be set aside as null and void by Divine law understood.

Of course students of material science shake their wise heads in derision at the idea of mental causation, but what does that prove?

Did not the persecutors of Galileo have to admit the truth of his discovery after they had tortured him for daring to state it?

Are not all discoveries of great principles treated in a similar fashion at first?

And have they not all withstood the assaults of the world that calls itself so highly civilized?

No great and mighty truths when once discovered can be wholly lost to the world.

Now, to dispose of this question of physical causation, science boldly declares there is no such thing in reality; what seems so is all in mortal belief, and it is the mortal belief in what is false that causes the mistakes in our life problem; the mistakes bring worry and failure, and finally sickness, sorrow and death as the world believes in death.

When it comes to putting the principles of science into practice as corrective measures, it is necessary to "lay the axe at the root of the tree," which, according to the teachings of Jesus, means to strike at the error that has caused the trouble, whatever it may be.

The first and gravest error of the race is the belief that the child of God is born of the flesh, according to the appetites of the flesh, and that every child that comes upon the scene has this belief deeply impressed upon it, and according to the laws of the flesh, both mind and body must suffer more or less in loss of health, vigor and vitality.

Hence the importance of righteous thinking and believing on the subject of the birthright of every child of God.

Even on the plane of the human intellect this law is acknowledged.

Deny that the yielding character of any child, either of its mind or body, renders it plastic to the mental influence under which it rests.

This is one of the denials made by Jesus Christ: "Call no man upon earth your Father."

So the claims of earthly parentage from first to last must be denied, whether made as claims of the flesh in appetites and passions or whatsoever.

By a denial of the claims of the flesh, you liberate the child of flesh from the mortal law.

If the mental atmospheres to which a child is subject are of a righteous character, it will show forth perfection in both mind and body, and the bent of its mind will be toward the good.

If the mental impressions are right in one way and wrong in another, there will seem to be righteous development in one direction and wrong in another.

All depends upon mental influences, even after the child becomes a man and thinks for himself.

By the term "righteous" we mean that which is right and true in every sense, not the sanctimonious idea of righteousness at all.

The sanctimonious Christian is never righteous; the very expression of the face proves the unrighteous character of his thoughts.

We say righteous thoughts, opinions and beliefs produce healthy and righteous effects.

In view of this statement we see how necessary it is to set the conscious mind in the way of truth, that its influence may correct all former errors and obliterate their effects.

To be thorough in the work of changing conditions from wrong to right, from evil to good, from sickness to health, etc., every one should begin with himself.

"Cast the beam out of thine own eye, that thou mayest see clearly to take the mote from thy brother's eye."

Begin at the very beginning and take up the

first and most demoralizing of all human errors, viz., the belief that a child of God could be brought forth from the flesh. Deny its reality first on the ground that it is of the devil, who is the parent of lies, and of all evil.

Nothing is true or real that proceeds from the devil, and only the carnal nature recognizes evil at all; so if we would have life and peace we must be firm in the rejection of all that opposes life and peace. Say to yourself in the silence, realizing only Spirit, There is no reality in lustful passions and sensual appetites.

Realize that Spirit is free from the claims of matter. Hold the thought with firmness and concentration for a time, then proceed with your mental argument.

The race beliefs in sensual appetites have no power over me, nor can they affect me in any way to my disadvantage.

Use any form of wording you choose that will embody the idea you wish to express and the impression you wish to make, or the response you wish to come forth.

Proceed in your denial of this error with deliberation, by taking up each avenue in detail through which we are all said to be liable to get impressions that are false.

The race, the ancestors and parents, the family and friends and the people you meet daily; also any individual you may have in mind as believed to be capable of exerting a bad influence, and your own false beliefs.

Declare that all beliefs in the lusts of the flesh from any source are powerless to hold you in bondage; powerless to darken your life, because they are false.

The power or potency of these words lies in the realization that the argument is true according to righteous reason, not according to sense evidence at all.

You can extend the argument with profit by taking up each individual feature of this error as it is manifest in the flesh and denying it vigorously.

It is all a delusion of the carnal nature.

Take up the belief in hereditary tendencies and reject its claim in the same manner.

You can inherit nothing in the flesh, and all such beliefs are mortal delusion.

"One is your Father which is in heaven."

So you can inherit only good. Claim it boldly.

This line of argument would be in the highest degree absurd if we were dealing with mortal law; but it must be understood that it is because morial law has claimed rule heretofore that we have these evil conditions and beliefs to overcome.

It must be understood also that it is by thinking and speaking only of spiritual perfection that we produce or show forth the perfect conditions upon our bodies and in our lives.

To think and believe in the flesh as real, and as having life and sensation, makes people selfish and sensual, and all these evil passions and miseries follow selfishness.

In the cleansing of your mind from error you can not be too thorough.

You must reason from the standpoint that admits nothing as true that does not accord with the allness of good and the supremacy of Spirit.

You base your argument on the statement that what is not true of Spirit is not true at all.

Your foundation is Christ (*Truth*), and "other foundation can no man lay."

When you have given yourself this cleansing by denial with earnestness and deliberation, you want to follow with affirmations of purity and goodness.

Clothe yourself as with a garment by devoutly acknowledging God as the great source of all goodness.

God is my life, therefore my life is free from impurity. God is my health, therefore I am healed of all discord. God is my strength, therefore I am free from all weakness of mind or body.

God is my wisdom, therefore I am free from all foolishness and mortal error.

All space is filled with life, health, strength, wisdom and love.

I live, move, and have my being in this Divine Omnipresent Good; therefore no evil can come to me; I am free, wise and immortal.

Such thoughts for self training establish trust and confidence in the proceeding, because they bring the peace and comfort that no other proceeding has ever done.

When the truth begins to seem practical to you, you will want to use the same argument for a patient or friend whom you wish to heal or reform; but you may feel very doubtful at first of your ability to use it with effect.

Those who have never observed the working of this wonderful law, are very apt to doubt at first that any such method can accomplish healing and reforming.

It seems like a strange proceeding, because we have always grovelled in the dust and ashes of materiality, and have never been taught the higher law till now.

Some think it might accomplish a *self*-reformation in morals, because of the purity of its principles; but how a cure can be effected upon another, or immoralities corrected by this silent proceeding, is a mystery.

Another doubter says, "If one can be reached by the process, why does it not accomplish the desired reformation in every case?"

This may be explained something after the manner of the parable of the sower, found in the XIII. Chapter of Matthew. The word is the seed, and it sometimes falls on stony ground. Sometimes among thorns which spring up and choke the good seed; but these are the obstacles we have to remove by denial. In many cases that fail to receive the good word, it is the hardness of heart which will not give up its cherished idols. The stony ground.

In other cases it is lack of patient perseverance with the word.

"The word of the Lord is as a hammer that breaketh the rock in pieces."

A lady came to one of our students who had been but three or four weeks in the understanding of this truth, begging her to treat her husband who was addicted to vice and dissipation in its worse forms, just as it seemed about to culminate in wrecking the home.

She treated continuously for three weeks by the denial of this error, followed by the affirmations of truth, at which time the wife reported a perfect reformation in every way.

He ceased from his drinking and gambling,

spent his evenings at home, and the old taste for former associations was gone.

She had laid the axe at the root of the trouble by the denial of that first error in which the carnal nature had held the child of goodness.

Success in this case was the result of earnest, determined perseverance.

It is faithful discipline that awakens a consciousness of the Christ within; and it is the Christ within that recognizes the Christ within our patient. It is not himself that does the wrong, and your righteous words arouse the true self to take the reins.

Let whatever you do be done in the name of *Christ Jesus.*

There is power in the very name.

"There is none other name under heaven given among men whereby we can be saved," but the name of Christ Jesus.

The whole Divine nature is embodied in the word Christ. It is written, "In Him is all the fullness of the Godhead bodily."

In His name we cast out evil tendencies.

In His name we teach this gospel of good news.

In His name we heal the sick by His command, and in proportion as we understand and live the law of righteousness as He taught it, will we manifest the Christ within us by doing the works He did.

We have access to all power through Him.

We may say the same as Paul, "I can do all things through Christ which strengtheneth me."

ANEURISM CURED.

A young lady suffering from an aneurismal tumor of the aorta, for which surgery and medication know no remedy, also suffering great prostration from imperfect heart action and nervous dread, living in constant anticipation of instant death, according to the predictions of doctors, was induced to avail herself of Divine Science treatment. She had one present treatment each day for a week. Then she was able to make a journey to friends a hundred miles away, and was treated absently for about a month; was perfectly well before the end of the month, and continues well and happy to-day. Patients healed by this truth are also healed of fear, and are always happier and more contented and satisfied afterward—satisfied with life.

LESSON VIII.

"Take heed that ye be not deceived."

UP to the present lesson, much has been said regarding mental influences, and the importance of knowing how every mind exerts more or less influence over other minds, whether present or absent; but more noticeable when present.

Any observing person will notice that he is consciously impressed with a feeling of depression and unrest in the presence of certain people, while the presence of others would be uplifting and pleasurable; all of which is due to the quality of the mind so affecting us.

Again, you may be seized with a feeling of depression and despondency, with no one present and with no conception at all of what causes it.

It has already been stated in substance that your mind is affected by such thoughts from outside sources as accord with your own peculiar beliefs and moods.

That is, you make yourself receptive to depressing thoughts from others by not holding to absolute truth yourself.

The mind that is anchored in absolute truth does not attract the false influences that depress and sadden it.

You will grow into knowing better than to allow any wrong thoughts from any source to disturb you; and as you grow in the knowledge of truth you will be able to cast off every belief of evil influence.

In time you will be able to know just what kind of minds affect you unpleasantly, and at the same time put its influence aside as powerless to harm you.

All such effects from other minds may be called personal influence, and should be met with righteous thoughts, which not only save you from unpleasant effects, but tend also to correct the error in them.

People of strong will, and lax ideas of right darken us and cloud our judgment if we allow it.

It is the false quality that radiates from such minds as are strongly wedded to mortal error, that reaches other minds, producing false conditions and destroying righteous judgment, which brings fear and conscious limitation.

People who talk of malicious animal magnetism, mesmerism and hypnotism, and believe in such power and fear it, make of themselves a magnet to attract such deceitful influences.

Even some who have long professed to believe in the allness of the Good, those who have started in as successful demonstrators of truth, and accomplished marvels of healing for a time, have been prevailed upon by personal influence, and so descended from righteous thinking as to join in calumnies and denunciation against those who do *not* harbor the monster called "malicious animal magnetism."

Scores of them have lost all power to demonstrate truth as they once did.

Truth is a jealous God, and will not divide honors.

What do all such influences amount to in reality? Nothing at all *in reality*, and what they amount to in *seeming* is just what we make of them by believing in them; nothing more.

We have only to look back upon the days of witchcraft and sorcery to remind us of what ignorance and superstition will do.

When people believed in witchcraft, it was not a difficult matter to find some object of aversion to suspect of having the powers to bewitch people.

The strange diseases and afflictions that could not be easily accounted for in other ways, were laid at the door of the poor old woman they called a witch.

She was shunned and hated and ostracized, until she reflected the malicious hatred; and every look and every move indicated the intensity of her malice, all of which increased the fear of her supposed powers.

No one ever suffered injury by her unless they believed in suffering. And when society reached a higher state of cultivation, the belief in witchcraft gradually died out, and people learned that ignorance and superstition were the magnets that drew the deceitful influences.

What is called malicious animal magnetism is just as false and foolish a delusion as old-fashioned witchcraft, and bears a strong resemblance to it in the way it is supposed to affect people.

To set up such a power in belief and give it a name, is to out-do the belief in a personal devil by many degrees.

He who allows himself to be persuaded into such belief will find himself in greater bondage than ever before.

Never harbor it for a moment; it is the falsehood that must be met by the command, "Get thee behind me"; and let the command be of no "uncertain sound."

To dally timidly with it betrays a fear of it.

We have no business to allow our minds to be open to such influences, which are always from minds in mortal error.

Any personal influence is liable to be deceptive, if not actually bad.

The only effect of association that is wholly reliable for good must be from the spiritually minded who put personality out of sight.

The truly spiritual in mind give us peace and rest by their presence. They inspire us with courage, and trust in the unseen Divine presence.

Avoid all strong personal attempts to control your views and opinions, and if you lack wisdom go to the great source of all wisdom.

Do as Job did. He grew weary of the advice of his conceited friends, and told them they were "all physicians of no value."

He said, "I would talk with God; I would reason with the Almighty." After which he was healed of his affliction, and with restored health came greater prosperity than ever before.

We may all reason with the Almighty by simply consulting the principles of Divine science, regardless of all personality.

When the judgment faculty is fully developed by righteous reasoning our eyes are opened to see how we may reason with the Almighty at all times.

If you have grasped the meaning of the statement of Divine Being, you realize that the Almighty embraces all goodness, truth, wisdom, intelligence and righteousness in the universe.

To reason in harmony with all that is good, wise, true and righteous in principle is the reasoning with the Almighty that makes you one with Divine Principle; and like Job you will find restored health, peace and prosperity, the result of your righteous reasoning.

The fact that error always counterfeits truth, and mortal mind simulates the ways of Immortal Mind, renders us liable to deceptions continually, until our judgment is quickened to detect the false.

Sense evidence seems to mortal mind the strongest evidence, and we hate to be convinced that it is deceiving.

When we first begin to deny the reality of matter we do it with much doubt and perplexity as to whether it is the right thing to do.

According to the senses matter seems the most real of all things, and we rebel against the absurd idea of denying its reality.

The mind is weighted with the belief in matter as long as we hold to it as real, and until we can boldly declare "there is no reality in matter" will the weight be lifted.

The persistent denial removes the weight. Some have been so lightened of their burdens that they were so dizzy at first as to be frightened, but they found upon the affirmation of Spirit as the only Substance, that great peace followed the practice.

There is nothing to fear, but a great deal to gain, by taking a bold, firm stand on the ground that Spirit is the only Substance.

When Jesus told his followers that the flesh profited nothing, and that Spirit was the only reality, many of them went away and walked no more with him.

They settled back into the old way of thinking, just about as some of our weak, half-hearted scientists do occasionally, when the seed has fallen upon stony ground.

When we consider that Jesus with his full and unreserved consecration to the ministry of Truth, did not always open their hearts to a full understanding, and did not always find his converts steadfast and true, we should not harbor despondency and discouragement because all do not stand firm to our teaching.

When Paul found some of the converts going back to their old ways, or showing indifference, he aroused them by the sharp command, "Awake, thou that sleepeth; arise from the dead; **awake to righteousness, and sin not.**"

He was urging them to shake off that indifference that makes them dead to the importance of holding righteous thoughts.

His admonition to "sin not" meant to make no compromise with error. Give it no quarter; reject it with decission, and stand by your convictions of truth; be not deceived by appearances.

Mortality will ever lead you into darkness and doubt if you follow its leading.

Deny its influence; reject every suggestion that does not accord with the infallible statement on which rests the whole law, viz., the absolute allness of the good; the omnipotence of the good and the omnipresence of the good.

By holding to this you cannot be deceived.

In the old sanctimonious way of approaching God, we were deceived into thinking we were unworthy of the blessings we payed for, and our prayers were made up very largely of admissions of depravity and sinfulness that we did not in reality believe a word of, and that we should have resented if any one else had dared to make such charges against us.

At the same time we believed God to be a God of justice, and we prayed for blessings that we were not entitled to according to our just deserts (as we believed); which was equivalent to asking God to deviate from His law of justice to oblige us.

Is it any wonder such Christians get no answers to their prayers?

They pray, and pray, and beseech God to relieve them of their distresses of mind and body, and when the relief does not come they generally conclude it is His will that they should suffer; and then they begin to pray for submission, but all the time yearning for relief—which is the real heartfelt desire, after all. No prayer for submission to evil conditions can ever be the real desire of the heart, and whoever believes so has not reasoned his way out of mortal error.

The prayer for submission brings you a feeling of dull, stupid discontent that makes you feel that life is not worth living; because you rise no higher in your conception of God than to suppose the gift of submission is the best He can do for you, and that false thought finds expression in your feeling of discontent.

The poetic quotation in third lesson applies right here again.

"Therefore the God that ye made you
   Was grievous, and brought you no aid;
Because it was by your false thought
   That the God of your making was made."

Every false thought regarding the nature and character of God is the making of a false God; and we have to think truly of God if we would have the true God work for us, and through us and with us, to the establishing of peace and harmony in our lives.

Only in knowing the *true* God we are made free.

The prayer for submission has never made people *love* sickness or sorrow or death, and never will.

This prayer of doubt and uncertainty is not the prayer of faith that saves the sick, but is the kind of praying that has been done for 1800 years *mostly*.

All Christendom as a body are praying daily (or every Sunday at least) for the kingdom of Satan to be overthrown, destroyed, and the kingdom of God to be established on the earth; and when Scientists begin to prove that it can be done, they call us blasphemers.

The God of their making is not able to carry out His righteous design.

Poor deluded mortals; deceived by a man-made creed, who ignorantly and unintentionally set at naught the teachings of the Christ they profess to follow, because they lack understanding of the application of His words to daily living.

Such a conception of God is purely a mortal conception.

Jesus said, "In vain do ye worship me, while

teaching for doctrines the commandments of men."

There are so many claimed ways for the credulous and unwary to be deceived by mortal error; so many avenues through which deceiving influences are said to reach them, that only a knowledge of truth can save them from the darkness that broods in ignorance.

It is knowledge of truth that makes us free.

In knowing truth we are able to put all deceiving influences under our feet.

In knowing the true way we think only true thoughts and speak only true words, and thus build the world around us as we desire, with wrong to no one.

Much has already been said regarding the power of the word.

Many who have been through the experience of using true words with understanding, and learned the power of the true word to liberate from sorrow and pain have declared that the memory, even of those old conditions, is like a dream.

No other method in all the world will lighten our burdens, or lift us out of despondency with such practical effects.

We may be absolutely free if we will throw out of the mind all the false beliefs and mortal deceptions that weigh us down, as you would throw ballast out of a balloon.

As the ballast is worthless except to weight the balloon and hold it down, so are the errors and deceptions worthless; they only weight us with sorrow and darken our pathway.

To deny their power lifts the weight and lets light on the path and gives us freedom.

Yet some are actually afraid of changing the old sorrowful life for one of freedom.

They have been warned so often of the danger of being too happy, they cling to the morbid belief that it is wicked to dare to be too much at peace.

If they find themselves enjoying life *too* well, even in the most rational and consistent manner, they will begin to invite sorrow unconsciously by self-reproach, as if God desired us to be miserable and we had no right to enjoy life.

All who live by such teaching, and allow their lives to be shadowed by such false ideas of God, are in bondage to the worst kind of deception.

We say the *worst*, because no deception could be worse than to be misled regarding the God on whom we depend for all things, and without whom we can have nothing.

This is another phase of bondage we have to break away from by denial.

What matter if you do feel strangely after denying the reality of evil, and matter? All is right as soon as you turn from the denial and affirm the ever present Divine love and freedom, and fully trust the one Divine power.

It should be remembered that our physical maladies are not always due to our own erroneous beliefs, but that impressions made in early childhood are often the cause of serious afflictions in later years.

A case in illustration is a gentleman of perhaps fifty years of age, who for many years was subject to very alarming attacks of acute inflammation, for which he had taken oceans of material medicines, and paid mints of money in his efforts to get well, all to no purpose.

A friend of the family, who had recently embraced these principles happened to call one day just as he was brought in from his office suffering agonies in one of his accustomed attacks. Being a friend, she begged the privilege of trying to relieve him, and while waiting for the doctor she treated him vigorously, relieving him of all pain in about fifteen minutes.

Her principal denial was fear of an angry God and a burning hell, as she afterward told me. He had not for years believed in any such thing himself, but admitted that in childhood he had suffered untold agonies of fear of the angry God and burning hell he heard so much about in Sunday school and in church.

The impression made upon his yielding body when too young to have any opinions of his own, had fruited in this condition that no drugs could reach, and as soon as that impression was removed he was relieved, and that was his last attack.

We find it necessary to take up each individual error of the race and every false idea and impression from parents and teachers, as well as the people we meet in daily life, call them by name, each in its turn, and deny its reality with all the vigor and vehemence the case seems to demand, and after denying its reality, deny the possibility of its effect upon you, to hold you in bondage.

When you take these words of discipline into your heart, determined to square your life by them, your judgment soon confirms the practice as wise, and your experience proves it.

Evil conditions will fall away like leaves in autumn, and you will remember them only as a dream.

Righteous judgment, perfect health, and new strength that comes as a result of this practice, makes you wonder why we should have been without this knowledge so long.

How patiently the good law has waited; how long it has stood ready to break down the walls of delusion between us and perfect health and peace!

How little the world has realized that the Christ is always with us, and always has been!

Only the truth can make us free, and only in this Divine Science can we know truth.

Only in Divine Science can we know or find the divine self.

Only in truth can we know the unreliability of mortal mind.

As the uncertain light of the moon is but a feeble reflected light, borrowed from the sun, so is the light or information obtained through mortal mind feeble and unreliable.

The warmth and vigor we get from the rays of the sun direct, is the type or symbol of the Divine intelligence, love and power that come from knowing the true self by righteous reasoning.

It wakes us from mortality into immortal freedom and blessedness.

We need to get all our light and strength from the true source or fountain head of light and strength.

We get this light and strength consciously by acknowledgment of the allness of the good, after the cleansing by denial.

As you denied the reality of the basic error made against the child of God and its effects in your first treatment of mind, so do you in the second attempt take up the denial of all deceitful influences from every quarter, remembering that only mortal mind deceives, and only mortal mind is deceived.

In mortal law no one is so easily deceived as the one who is deceitful.

If you are deceitful in your mortal nature, that nature acts as a magnet to attract deceitful influences, by which you are constantly being deceived, and thus living on the ragged edge of uncertainty in all your undertakings.

Deceitfulness is the devil to be cast out in this case.

As you have cleansed your own mind of deceitfulness, and also of the possibility of being deceived, and you have accomplished it by the process of denying the false and affirming the true, you see the wisdom of treating a patient or friend in the same manner; let it be sickness, sorrow, ill temper or whatever, the process is the same—*make them nothing*.

When you have thoroughly and deliberately obliterated the effects of passions and appetites, and all hereditary beliefs regarding this error, with understanding of why you do it, you want to forget it; set it aside as a conquered delusion, and never refer to it again, lest you invite its delusive influence again.

You do the same when treating a patient or friend; hold firmly and persistently to the denial until you feel you have removed the error, then hold as firmly to the affirmation of the truth you wish to establish and refer no more to the error.

All the evil passions and immoral traits you deny are the result of false impressions that come to us from all sides and from every quarter regarding the processes and consequences of all that pertains to physical existence; the evidence of sensation, which deceitful influences are continually reporting falsely and forcing the intellect to agree to it.

In this process we train the intellect to reject this false testimony, and to consciously realize that we are never without the inner light of our own unseen divine being; the light that lighteth every man that cometh into the world; the true schoolmaster; the unerring counsellor.

By depending upon this unerring guide we set ourselves free from the deceitful influences that are perpetually whispering with their five mortal voices telling us that sensations are true, while the silent monitor tells us they are *not* true.

It is these five mortal voices that keep us constantly in terror of some evil happening, and while listening to any one of them, we can never attain to purity of heart.

We *see* the evil, we *hear* the evil, we *feel* the evil effects of judging by sense evidence. We even taste and smell impurity, while to be pure in heart (which is to rise above the mortal conceptions that deceive), we shall see and know only the good.

"Only with thine eyes shalt thou see and behold the reward of the wicked."

Blessed testimony to the unreliability of sense evidence; therefore take heed that ye be not deceived, but rise on the sweet words of Truth by rejecting all error.

BRIGHT'S DISEASE CURED.

A gentleman whom the physicians had pronounced incurable was sent as a last hope to a famous resort for invalids to try the mineral waters for the kidney trouble. After using the waters for several weeks faithfully, all the time growing worse and worse, he happened to hear of patients who were being healed of this, that and the other by the teachers of Science at one of the hotels. Knowing that doctors nor drugs could do anything more for him, he decided to try this new plan, whatever it was.

His appearance on the occasion of his first call was of one thoroughly discouraged, dejected and miserable. The constant irritating pain in the kidneys gave him a look of despair which seemed almost like a cry of agony, and for months this had been his experience daily.

He was treated twice daily when present and was given instruction for self-treatment, after which he went away healed. He afterward admitted by correspondence that he was healed at the second treatment. All pain left during the treatment with a wave of peace, and he has continued well for three years. He refrained from acknowledging it at the time for fear it would not be permanent.

LESSON IX.

"Let your communications be yea, yea, and nay, nay; for whatsoever is more than these cometh of evil."

LET it be understood that your denials and affirmations are the nay, nay and yea, yea of scripture. You want to be definite in your denials, and definite with your affirmations.

First convince yourself of what is true, and then stand so firm that the gates of hell shall not prevail against you.

Any ifs or buts, or doubts or wavering, are not yea, yea, or nay, nay.

Any contention or controversy is of the letter, and not of the Spirit; therefore it cometh of evil, of error.

Put aside all desire to prove *your* way of thinking correct, and let the light of Divine wisdom shine upon you to the exclusion of any selfish desire.

"Then will your light break forth as the morning, and your health shall spring forth speedily."

A very prevalent error among people who have not studied the principles of the Science of Mind is in supposing that the healing power is the most important of its ministrations. The very fact that our bodily ills are cured, and all kinds of physical infirmities healed, tends to attract those who consider their fleshly conditions paramount to all else.

When the student begins to *understand*, he will see that perfect health, strength and freedom are a sure and natural outcome or result of knowing and accepting the principles.

Those whose motives and aims are no higher than to secure healing for the body, are generally very slow to realize health; while the one who takes up the study for the grand truths it teaches, and loves it for very righteousness sake, will get well without an effort.

Health and strength steal upon them so gently that they hardly know when the change takes place.

Some who have been great sufferers for years have been restored to perfect health in a few days by simply listening to the lessons and drinking in the freedom that each lesson teaches.

When the majesty and glory of these principles first dawns upon the consciousness, there is healing in the very contemplation of it.

The mind that realizes and acknowledges the perfect law is open to receive the benefit of it.

Full acknowledgment of its power and trust in its potency is the magnet that attracts the principle of health and peace.

The one who thinks only of what he will gain for the flesh, or for some material circumstance will often wait days and weeks for results that might be reached without delay, if he would only let the Spirit of truth reign supreme without question as to how it shall work.

"It is the spirit that quickeneth."

We need to be strongly at one with the words of truth; strongly at one with the principles we claim to understand and endorse, if we would have perfect results follow our efforts, and if we would grow and strengthen in powers.

One who thinks only of the cure for his body is not one with Divine Principle, and while he is so intent upon the cure for his body, he is very apt to think a little dose of something else will expedite the cure, or that it will hasten matters if he takes great care of his body, and is very prudent about what he eats and drinks, and about taking cold and other habits; all of which betrays a lack of confidence and trust in the Divine power he claims to consult and rely upon.

"Commit thy way unto the Lord; trust also in him, and he will bring it to pass."

No other remedies and no other system of cure agrees with the Science of Mind in a practical way, and any attempt to mix it with other remedies, or other methods, is like serving two masters.

Divine law works without material aids, and only requires recognition and acknowledgment.

The Divine law of cure is the Christ cure, and no one ever heard of Jesus Christ giving poisons or powders to expedite a cure.

No one ever heard of his warning his patients to be careful about their diet, or about taking cold, or about malaria, or seeking a better climate; no such ideas ever entered into his ministry.

He simply said, "Thy sins are forgiven thee," meaning, "For error (which is sin) I give you truth."

His very presence radiated truth, and the strong impressions from his pure mental presence made the sick rise in perfect health.

We can all do the same; we *ought* all to do the same, for the same possibility rests in every soul.

To abide in truth makes the truth cure possible to all.

The truth cure is the Christ Cure, and all lack of confidence or trust in the Christ method of cure may be laid at the doors of ignorance, or of false education, which amounts to the same.

The study of these principles will be of no avail unless you trust them. To make them practical in your life, you need to abandon all dependence upon old methods and material aids, and trust absolutely to Divine law.

In ignorance of truth we suppose we are subject to many dangers which, when we *know* truth, we find are mere phantoms.

In ignorance of truth we suppose we are at the mercy of the elements, and with this supposition we are afraid.

Thus in the cold, in the heat, in the storm, and in the flood we have no abiding place secure from danger.

Fear like a monster of reality takes us captive, and we forget the promise to him that "dwelleth in the secret place of the most high," which simply means an abiding trust in Divine Principle.

In that secret place you are hid from all danger; no evil can approach you; no plague can come nigh you; "at pestilence and famine you shall laugh." You are even "hid from the scourge of the tongue," and you may put all difficulties under your feet; you find there is nothing to fear.

All fear comes from believing in danger.

The first emotion of the human mind or human race recorded in Genesis is that of fear.

When the Lord God called Adam to account the first time, he answered from his hiding place saying, "I heard thy voice in the garden, and I was afraid."

Fear comes of disobedience, and according to the Allegory, Adam had willfully disobeyed the law of God.

The voice of God which he heard in the garden was the prompting of his divine nature to obedience and loyalty to the good.

The voice of God in every instance is the prompting of the divine within us, to turn from error to truth; to turn from mortality's claims to the real and true.

The false claim of the mortal in this case is the belief in danger; hence the fear. We are afraid because we believe we have sinned, done wrong, gone astray *as a race*, not as individuals, but as a race totally depraved and subject to danger on very hand.

The race believes in original sin, and in the depravity that prompts dishonesty and fraud; therefore every man is on the alert; he is afraid of being wronged.

He seems not to know that his fear of wrong

reaches his neighbor *unconsciously*, and is liable to set him to planing the very wrong he fears.

Men legislate and enact laws for the suppression of fraud and dishonesty, (with the best of intentions no doubt,) and every such law is made with the supposition that men need the restraining influence of the law. The enactment of the law is because of the universal belief in man's depravity, and the universal belief in man's depravity is continually prompting men to break the law, and the criminal is blamed and ostracised for falling into the error of violating the law, while the fault all lies in the ignorance of the law makers, who ought to understand the responsibility of mental action in the formation of popular beliefs regarding men and the ways of men. Many an honest servant has been suspected of dishonesty, and has been watched with suspicion for weeks and months, and held so constantly under the thought of theft that the impression made by the suspicion became too strong, and he or she finally fell when there was no natural tendency to dishonesty at all.

God speed the day when the balance of mental power is acknowledged by all men to be on the side of righteous thinking; when all will be moved to spontaneous deeds of love and charity, and honesty reign without reference to man-made laws; when all will recognize the law of God, the law of Love as Omnipotent, and no fear will cloud the judgment and cause men to fall into crime because of the mortal belief in evil.

Fear is very closely allied to selfishness, and selfishness may be said to be the root of all the secret sins of the race.

Pride, envy, jealousy, hatred, malice and deceit all arise from selfishness.

Selfishness leads to pride, and pride to envy, and envy to jealousy, and so on down to malice, revenge and cruelty, in all of which fear plays a very prominent part.

The fear of being deprived of some right or privilege is degrading and demoralizing, and breeds hatred, aversion and contempt.

A very common complaint of young students when they first begin their self training is that they have a bad temper; and they want to know how they can learn to control the bad temper. They seem to know intuitively that their uncontrolled temper has been, and *is*, their worst enemy.

Now let us reason this qnestion. All that you have and all that you are, is God given. God never gave you anything that is not good; and God never gave you a bad temper. Then how is it?

Why, according to reason you have no such thing as a bad temper; according to appearance you *have*, but it is all a mortal delusion which you will never conquer till you go at it scientifically.

Deny it most emphatically, but don't imagine that the denial is a license to indulge the passion. Not at all.

The belief in a bad temper is productive of great misery on a mortal plane, and is a false belief.

Put it under your feet; it has no claim to fellowship at all. Know that God is Peace, Omnipresent peace, and if you abide in truth nothing can ruffle your temper.

God is Love, and if you abide in Love there can be no anger.

The same may be said of all the secret sins that come of selfishness.

Any feeling of anger, hatred, aversion or suspicion has its root in selfishness, and can only be cured by love.

By honest candor you can soon conquer all hatred or aversion by righteous reasoning.

To abide in truth and keep the true word will set you free from every secret sin and its effects in seeming.

How to **abide in truth** and love, is with many

the point that seems impractical, while in reality it is very simple.

Let all your arguments for truth be based in the one statement of Divine Being, which admits of no reality in anything which contradicts that statement; therefore you are to deny every evil passion that is contrary to the law of love, or to the allness of the good.

Remember the power of the word. If you deny selfishness in all its phases with a conscious realization of the law of love, you put all selfish impulses under your feet, and let Divine Love take its place; then you abide in love and peace.

To secure harmony in all your life conditions, you will see the wisdom of gaining the mastery over all evil thoughts and unholy passions, as well as all dependence upon material props or medicinal aids in sickness.

As you have already accepted the statement that "there is but one power," be consistent, and stand by that statement.

Your power for good consists in your steadfast loyalty to that statement; while to turn back to the belief that a senseless drug has power for good nullifies your trust in Divine Law, and you lose the healing effect.

"Thou shalt have no other Gods before Me." Truth is a jealous God, and cannot tolerate error.

If your eye is single to the truth, your whole body will be full of light, which is equivalent to saying, if you are loyal in your trust of Divine Law, perfect harmony of body will be the result. It is not till the mind thinks and acknowledges absolute truth that things will be seen in their true light.

The conscious mind is the believing agent, and while it rises no higher than believing, it is still mortal.

It proves itself mortal by believing false statements, but when it is trained to *know* instead of believe, it is born again.

It drops the mortal and puts on immortality, and *knows* it is divine.

While in the mortal believing state, it is simply a sign, or a shadowing forth of the divine faculties of the spiritual self.

Every movement of the conscious mind in the believing state, signals some divine idea of which it is the shadow.

The conscious mortal mind or human intellect takes the shadow, the body, for the substance, and thinks and talks only of the shadow, till it is born into the knowledge that Spirit is the only Substance.

It is better to cease speaking or thinking of the mortal as the man; the mortal appearance is not the man at all.

It is not the image and likeness of God because it *is* mortal, and because it changes and perishes.

It is not the image and likeness of God in that it has no life or intelligence.

"All flesh is as grass; the grass withereth, the flower fadeth, but the word of the Lord endureth forever."

The word of the Lord is the word of truth, and when we speak of the flesh as *man*, we speak untruth, and the flesh makes the lie manifest in disease and discord.

"If we sow to the flesh, we reap corruption."

As we think and believe, so do we build the fleshly shadow; and if we think and talk only of that which is eternally the image of God when thinking or speaking of man, the flesh will take on health, and all things will partake of the deathless character of our thoughts and words.

Jesus said that his words were Spirit, and they were Life, and he also said, "If a man keep my saying he shall never see death."

To keep his sayings we shall be consciously liberated from the fear of death; we shall be one with eternal life, therefore we shall never see death.

The mind must be confidently anchored in this knowledge of the real and true before peace will abide with us, and before we can do the best thing for ourselves or our neighbors.

When you are wise enough to see that the conscious mortal mind is nothing of itself, and the conscious mind is willing to relinquish its claim to responsibility, and willing to admit its unreliability in and of itself, you have reached the meek and lowly state in which spiritual judgment shines forth and you see what you are.

You have rejected the claims of mortal mind and the evidence of sensation so perfectly that you actually do not hear them; you ignore them so completely that you are the destroying law against them.

The very fact that you know and declare them false renders them null and void to you.

All changes from error to truth and all removal of falsity wait the words of conscious mind.

In the story of the creation God said, "Let the waters bring forth." "The waters" symbolize the conscious mind of man, and as we are now dealing with the question of health we may say, "Let the conscious mind bring forth health-giving thoughts."

There is a belief that weighs heavily upon the hearts of men, that all evil conditions come upon us because of sin; and no one has ever explained that sins are mistakes or errors of judgment because of trusting to mortal law; but all believe sin to be wicked and wilful violation of true law; and each individual expects to be visited with the penalty according to law, and so lives in a state of mortal bondage to fear.

Every individual who believes in his own innate depravity will feel the coils of mortal law tighten about him with each year of his life (as he believes). He grows old in the belief that misery and pain are the inevitable portion of mankind, and every twinge of pain, every anxious fear, seems to him to be making ready to spring death upon him as a punishment for being born depraved.

He yearns for deliverance; he prays for deliverance; he begs for mercy, and yet he believes his misery to be a part of the plan of his heavenly Father.

Monstrous delusion!

Such are the false beliefs of the most highly-civilized portions of Christendom, and such are the impressions we have to erase.

Jesus said, "Every plant that my heavenly Father has not planted shall be rooted up."

It will be remembered that the first step in our cleansing discipline in seventh lesson was the rooting up of the beliefs in heredity according to the flesh and the fear that accompanies all falsity,

The second step in eighth lesson was the rooting up of all deceitful personal influences and the accompanying fears.

We come now to the third step in our cleansing discipline, which embraces all the secret sins of the race; all of which should be taken deliberately, each one by its name, and denied with vigor and firmness.

All are of the devil, hence all are false.

The great sin (error) of the world is selfishness, and when selfishness has been rooted up from each individual character, then will man love God supremely and his neighbor as himself, and the whole law will be fulfilled.

Begin with this final cleansing discipline as you did in seventh lesson, denying selfishness of every shade and degree through all the five avenues. Be thorough, deliberate and determined to root it out.

Specify the different shades of selfishness and secret sins; call every one by name—pride, envy, jealousy, hatred, malice, revenge and cruelty—and after denying their reality, deny that any belief from any source regarding their influence or effect can have any power to harm yourself or anybody you know. Declare that *there is no power in evil*, and you are not afraid.

Then take up prejudice, criticism, superstition,

calumny, censure and suspicion. Treat the same way. Deny the power of any of these things to move you, or trouble you, or hurt you. You reason always from the same standpoint, viz., the allness of the good.

From that standpoint you see how impossible it would be for calumny, or suspicion, or criticism, or hatred, or malice, or envy, to do any harm, because they have no power where the omnipotent Good is acknowledged.

After these denials do as before. Devoutly affirm the good that is the opposite of every false thing you have denied.

Make love your principal affirmation, because love is the fulfilling of the law. Love heals. Love comforts. Love blesses. Love is God, and Love fills all space, and where Love is there can be no selfishness. Love is peace. Love is harmony. God is all, and God is Love.

As a closing thought of assurance to yourself say, "My word shall not return to me void."

CANCER HEALED.

A lady suffering from uterine cancer of the most distressing and offensive character, whose physicians had declared she could live but a short time, and whom no medicine would relieve even temporarily, was healed perfectly sound and well in ten days by treatments and lessons combined. Her complexion, which was of a dead leaden hue, was completely transformed in a few days, showing a healthy glow and natural beauty.

Every vestige of the tumor was gone, and the incessant pain had given place to peace and rest, such as she had not dared to hope for again.

After two years of trust in Divine Law she continues a vigorous, healthy woman, with no fear of sickness to weigh her down and no dread of a return of her old trouble, because she rests in a knowledge of truth.

LESSON X

"Perfect love casteth out fear."

SOMETIMES the student of Divine Law as he goes deeper and deeper in the study of its principles, and is more and more impressed with the grandeur of the theme, is tempted to go back to the contemplation of Christianity as it seemed to him before he knew this truth, and he is quite startled to find so many of the old landmarks completely washed away.

He sees what a complete turning about from the old ideas, and old ways the science teaches, and if he is not firm and strong to resist the tempter he will begin to yield to the fear of being misled.

This tempter is ever ready to lead you back to the old, dark, helpless ways again, and your anxiety (which is another phase of error) will cloud your judgment as before, and make you forget that those old, dark, false ways have never brought you anything but confusion and discord, and by those ways you never found relief from your physical difficulties, nor your mental troubles, nor how to help your friends out of such conditions.

People are too prone to consider the way their Father and Grand-Father believed in, the only righteous way. No matter how absurd their religious views may have been, or how little judgment was brought to bear upon their ways, we are apt to allow those early impressions to outweigh all reasoning, unless we plant our feet firmly on the rock Christ, Truth, and know for ourselves what is righteous reasoning.

No matter how sincere our parents were in their beliefs, they all labored under the same darkness of error from which the world would never emerge if all should persist in holding fast to the old ways and travel in the same old ruts because the parents and grandparents did.

We are no more in duty bound to believe in and respect false opinions regarding God and religion because our parents did, than we would be to retain and imitate the dishonest and immoral traits of parents.

The only way to rise above the effects of all mortal error, is to know truth for ourselves, regardless of what any mind in mortal error (in the past or present) may say, and when once you *know* what is true, you will find a way to make the Principle work for you if you are willing to trust it.

You have already learned the mysterious power of the law, if you have been faithful with your discipline.

The method of using the law or setting the beautiful principle, Truth, to work for you has all been explained, and you have proved the wonderful potency of denials to put all obstacles out of your way, and all difficulties under your feet, and you know you can deny the power of anything to oppose you in what is right.

Nothing can stand in your way if you so declare it.

You begin to realize the power in true words, you begin to think more in harmony with righteous law; and to your surprise you will find your desires have undergone a complete change in character.

Things do not look as they did from the old standpoint, and you wonder you ever had such fancies, and you are glad those foolish desires were not gratified, because you see it would never have satisfied you at all to have things as you once thought you wanted them.

With your enlightened judgment the real and satisfactory way is opened, and you smile to think of that old groveling desire.

In every such experience you climb to a higher plane. Every time you gain the mastery over even the smallest problem you are better fitted for greater ones, and you will soon be convinced that the principles of science are your only remedy in every emergency.

All students when first dealing with these principles are liable, now and then, to feel that they do not understand or know just how to proceed in certain cases; things look very dark at such times. All the old beliefs are taken away, and they feel strange, uncertain and restless. They see that all the hard, cold discouragements they have to encounter, and all the misery and wretchedness they see in the world, and the doctrines they have held so sacred, are all a flat contradiction of these beautiful statements; and how to reconcile this scientific reasoning with what seems so real and so contradictory is the question.

Don't try to reconcile them; it can't be done.

They cannot be made to harmonize, and the more you hesitate and waver the longer you put off the day of deliverance.

The benefits you derive from science will be in exact proportion to your loyalty to the principles of science.

By just so much as you believe in and trust

the science have you turned your back upon the old beliefs in error, and just in that proportion will you prove the science true.

If you find yourself doubting your ability to conquer any seeming difficulty, you know the law, and you know the way to make it work for you.

Deny the doubt vigorously; put it under your feet. It is a negative condition that has no claim to consideration at all. *There is no doubt.*

Then serve your belief in inability the same way. Be vigorous and persistent with these denials till you feel that you *are* able.

Say to yourself, "I can do all things through Christ which strengtheneth me."

Say to yourself daily till you rise above the need of constant discipline, "There is no power in ignorance to darken me; there is no power in evil to harm me, and there is no substance in matter to hinder me; for God is my wisdom, God is my refuge, and God is omnipresent Spirit."

Faith in this principle is not demanded of you in blindness. Your reason tells you it is true, the Scriptures teach us the same truth, and Jesus Christ declared it to be the only saving truth, and none who deny it can possibly be true followers of Christ.

All the miracles and mighty deeds recorded in

Scripture were accomplished in mental action by the intense and absorbing realization of good as the only reality; and every individual of ordinary intelligence is capable of accomplishing similar good works by the same devotion to Principle in mental action.

It is the intense realization of what is true that sets the law to work in making the good manifest in all our environments.

The greater the unity of sentiment among the people in this realization of good, the greater will be the manifestation in every department of human experience, until the influence for good will reach every soul who does not close his mind against the truth by harboring mortal error.

All error is the opposite of truth, and it is no more entitled to consideration because your church and your ministers endorse it than the error held by the most pronounced infidel.

Those who are called infidels generally believe as they do because they see none of the fruits of Godliness manifest among those who profess Godliness.

The creeds of Christendom virtually deny the power of God to work among men as they freely admit it *once* did; and at the same time declare that God is the same yesterday, to-day and forever; and that His promises are sure; but with most remarkable perversity they put off the fulfillment of most of the promises for the world to come.

Even the holy prophets, as they are called, could only see what was possible in the fulfillment of the law; except in rare instances, when the Divine light dawned upon them with sufficient glory to reveal what they could accomplish in the *now*.

They generally foretold what would be at some future time, and it remained for Jesus of Nazareth to teach the people of the *now*. He never postponed, as the prophets did. He came to fulfill, and it was always *now* with Him.

He never exhorted people to prepare for death, but came that they might have life, and have it more abundantly.

Abundant life is impossible to those who persist in the error that finds its ultimate in death. The life forces are in the ascendant (even on the physical plane) with all who accept the Christ in the spirit of truth.

He said, "I am the way, the truth and the life."

He meant to imply that His life, His works and His teaching was the way for all to follow.

By truly believing and following Him we shall do the same works He did.

The power is with every one *now*, and is only hidden from conscious realization by mortal beliefs in what is false.

Those mortal beliefs are the lies which the prophet declares have been spoken every man to his neighbor. He said "they have made lies their refuge," and he foretold the coming of the word of truth which should sweep away the refuge of lies, but he failed to see that the power to accomplish the same was inherent in himself, so he put it off. He postponed the day of salvation, as all prophets have done, but which we now find is not the Christ teaching.

He came to fulfill the law, according to prophecy, and He left the command with all His followers to do as He did, which is to fulfill *now*.

We begin to *know* what our powers are by denying and completely obliterating the false ways and false impressions we have heretofore allowed to darken our lives.

We accomplish wonderful things by knowing and boldly declaring that all evil is delusion.

No other belief of a religious or reformatory character in the world has ever accomplished such results in healing, and blessing and reforming.

"By their fruits ye shall know them."

Every faithful student of truth will find after

reasoning for a time in this line, that there will be a complete overturning of his character, his thoughts and his aims in life.

The practice of denials is the washing process which sometimes brings the error you deny out in greater prominence than before; only for the time, however.

It is the nature of the law to uncover and bring to the surface what you have kept hidden (unconsciously, perhaps) even from yourself.

For instance, if you have kept envy or jealousy in a secret recess of your heart, and you have practiced your discipline in good earnest, in which all such evil passions are included in your denials, do not be surprised to find envy or jealousy springing up in the most glaring fashion.

It comes to the surface, and shows fight like a thing of life, because you have routed it from its hiding place.

It is well for it to do so in many cases, as it gives you a hint of what you need to do.

It has to be dealt with vigorously and with firmness and decision.

Erase it at once, and affirm your freedom, and if you are thorough and steadfast it will never show forth again; and if you are wise you will never refer to it again even in thought. "Forget the things which are behind," and reach forward to those which are before, as we are admonished by the Apostle Paul.

It is a great hindrance to your growth in the understanding of the way of life to refer to past errors, past injuries, past sorrows or pains; they should all be dropped into the well of oblivion, forgotten and ignored forevermore, if you would remain free.

It is also unscientific to discuss the shortcomings or failings or sicknesses of others; by talking of them you augment the evil because you fellowship with it, and that is all the encouragement it wants.

If you hear of the dangerous illness of a neighbor, don't go to your other neighbors and spread the intelligence, but mentally deny the whole account. Every individual who hears or knows of the condition of that patient, and thinks of him as dangerously ill, helps to hold illness there, helps to bind the coils of mortal law the closer.

The anxious fears of parents and friends in case of illness often bear so heavily upon the patient that it dies for no other reason than that it was smothered with fear and anxiety; all because of ignorance of Divine law, which all may know if they will.

When children are watched with anxious care, and cautioned and continually reminded of the awful reality of evil, and the danger from evil associations, and covered with fears that they may fall into vice and immorality, they are all the more liable to fall into temptation; while to hold them in mind as strong in righteous character, and give thoughts of confidence, and trust in the promptings of their better self, will lead them away from temptation and make them love the good.

The anxiety and care bestowed upon our children, and upon the friends we love, though prompted by the best of motives, is proved by mortal experience to be unwise if not absolutely demoralizing.

We have been educated to consider it a virtue rather than a wrong to be constantly looking for something to correct, something to reprove in children.

Is it any wonder they so often go astray? Without some strong counter-influence they could not help it.

The belief in the inherent depravity of man; the belief in the reality and power of evil, and the man of flesh as the actual man, has been for ages a fixed conclusion of mortal mind; and the mind of man may drift hither and thither, upon this wave and that wave, and change its opinions at will, on subjects that weigh very lightly compared with this great problem of life, and yet, it *will* cling to this monstrous error which is the parent of all misery.

As long as the human family persist in such error, so long will the race have to pay the penalty in afflictions and discords.

The Psalmist David said that, "Fools, because of their transgressions, and because of their iniquities, are afflicted." And Solomon said that, "Fools *die* for want of wisdom."

There is an axiom in Metaphysics which reads, "Every bodily condition and organ is the translation into outward manifestation of some fixed way of thinking."

Now, if we have a fixed belief that depravity or degeneracy is inherent in our natures, there must be a translation of that belief into *some* department of our lives; and according to the law of correspondence any *false* way of thinking when it becomes fixed in the mind will eventually show forth in disease of body, mental inharmony or unhappy surroundings.

Any attempt to prove in what way certain errors will affect certain organs or circumstances, or in what way certain false beliefs will show forth, will only fail, because no fixed law can be made to work on a false basis; we can never tell what an error is going to lead to, because it *is* an error.

So in mortal mind we can never tell what false beliefs, or evil passions, or what combination of falsity has caused the tumor, the carbuncle, or whatever.

Mortal mind only deals with mortality, and never knows what is true of the spiritual man, and it remains for the child of Science alone to detect causes. Only in science can we become spiritually minded.

By a knowledge of truth the intuition is quickened, and it springs to our aid in every emergency.

Intuition is direct apprehension or cognition of a Truth. It is a perception of Truth without the process of audible reasoning; and you will often be intuitively impressed with the error you need to deny most vigorously in your own discipline, or in treating a patient, and you will deal with it accordingly.

We come now to the fourth movement, or the fourth step in the process of changing old, false beliefs for knowledge of what is true.

You have obliterated all false beliefs regarding appetites, deceit and selfishness and secret sins of every description; and in doing so you have disturbed the old settled convictions of your mind. You had been thinking in a certain way about life and the ways of life, and the part you as an individual had to play in the drama of life; and you find that this scientific reasoning does not agree with your old ideas of life.

You see that the scientific reasoning is true, and that to live by the principles of the true science you must turn about, because these principles dispute every one of those old false beliefs.

A rebellious feeling comes up which tempts you to go back to the old way, but reason says, "Stand by the principles of Science, because you know they are true"; there is a conflict going on, and mortal mind does not like to yield.

What is the conflict about?

In this case we will say you have believed in the great prevailing error of the race; you believe that although you are supposed to be a child of God, you are very wicked and depraved; you think you are a doer of evil, and desperately wicked. That God has the power and the will to punish you forever, and that you are powerless to help yourself.

No conviction of mortal mind is more firmly fixed, rooted and grounded, than that we have all done wickedly, and that we must suffer the consequences.

This belief in guilt is the falsity that works the greatest harm of all; yet the human mind clings to that belief, and thinks it wrong and dangerous to deny it, although it is a blind law that could only spring from ignorance, and the danger is in retaining that belief.

"Whoever believes in blind law, blindly believes he has broken a law."

The miserable savage is just as wretched when he believes he has offended his God of wood or stone.

To this deep and intense conviction of guilt in your mind, you have in your third treatment brought a direct and positive denial. You have given a flat contradiction to what you believed was true regarding the secret sins and selfish propensities of your heart.

The result of that discipline is now showing forth in a state of mind bordering upon anger. You have faced your worst enemy in those denials, and there is a conflict going on which no one can decide but yourself.

You are afraid of your enemy, and you hardly know whether to agree with it and let it hold the reins, or denounce it and take control yourself.

This is the trial of your faith. It is the fermentation caused by the word of truth coming in contact with an obstinate error. The error has held the fort so long it will not yield without a conflict, and it makes a battle ground of your conscious mind and body, making you nervous, confused and wretched.

Sometimes all the old diseases and all the pains of your past life will seize upon you in the most unexpected manner.

If you have been treating yourself for some disease of the body, you are liable to forget all about your disease and wonder what new complication you are called upon to suffer. It is no longer your disease that ails you when this crisis comes; it is what is called in science *chemicalization*, and in this stage of the case the principal trouble is fear—guilty fears; fear of punishment, fear of being worse, fear of death, fear of every conceivable evil.

Sometimes in this crisis there is very great suffering; sometimes very little. Sometimes no pain at all, but great mental depression; sometimes all the evil tempers will spring forth like so many demons, and the patient will be irritable, cross and disagreeable beyond all endurance. Now, dear student, you will be very glad to know that this condition is only temporary in any case, and need not come to any if the affirmations are given with perfect trust after the denials of evil passions and false beliefs.

Every treatment given by first denying evil passions should be followed by the most comforting words of affirmation, and it is well to deny the possibility of any disturbance, and follow it by the affirmation of love and peace.

Sometimes the chemicalization *will* seem to come in spite of all precaution. So you will need to know how to deal with it.

You will be able to conquer the *worst* conditions if you conquer the fear.

Let your treatment be very soothing in thought; you can give your thoughts the same tone as you would your words.

Say very gently (in thought) to yourself or your patient, "There is nothing to fear. You are not afraid and I am not afraid." You make this denial gently and soothingly.

If you have been treating for some special disease, you do not refer (even in thought) to the disease, but just deny the present appearance and the fear and guilt and whatever seems to disturb; then say to your patient or yourself, as if explaining (mentally) why these symptoms are false,—You are Spirit, a child of God made in His image and after His likeness. You live, move and have your being in God, therefore you cannot suffer pain or confusion. You are at peace; God is your peace, God is love. He covers you with His love as with a garment. His life is lived within you. God is your life.

Repeat your comforting affirmations till you feel that you have clothed your patient with the garment of peace and wholeness, and always pronounce the patient whole *now;* always *now.*

It is quite common for an inexperienced practitioner to become alarmed when a patient seems chemicalized; but remember there is nothing to fear, and if you allow fear the mastery, you can do nothing for your patient. First conquer your own fear, and then do the same for your patient. The way *you* feel he is sure to demonstrate.

This is the time of all others when you want to be firm and fearless.

Since you *know* there is no reality in pain, never let any such condition frighten you.

Chemicalization is simply the process which conscious mind and physical body undergo by being aroused to a consciousness of the need of taking a true base in thought, and there has to be a dissolution or destruction of old false conditions before the new basis can be reached.

It is called chemicalization because it is so perfectly symbolized by the process which chemicals go through in the change from one condition to another to recombine and produce new compounds, as in the case of wine or cider, which has a muddy, impure appearance until it goes through this chemicalization, after which the liquid is clear and pure.

Every patient or student who goes through this cleansing experience comes out with purer morals, keener judgment and perfect health of body.

In many cases the old care-worn expression gives place to a radiant bloom that amounts to a perfect transformation in a few days; even the complexion will become clear, and the freshness of youth will be felt as well as manifest in outward appearance, according to the promise spoken through the prophet Isaiah. "They that wait upon the Lord shall renew their strength; they shall mount up on wings as eagles, they shall run and not be weary, they shall walk and not faint."

The children of the science are daily proving this prophecy in a literal sense as well as in the deeper spiritual significance. Let it be remembered that every such change toward perfect bodily conditions is accomplished by changing the opinions, beliefs and emotions of the mind without regard to the body at all. Your body stands in the same relation to your conscious mind, that the barometer does to the weather.

The weather is not in the least dependent upon the barometer, nor affected by it. The barometer simply indicates the quality and condition of the atmosphere, as your body indicates the character and tone of your thoughts, beliefs and opinions.

When this crisis we call chemicalization comes, the body indicates the tumult caused by contradicting the fixed beliefs of the mind. There was some especial error in the mind that was more obstinate and determined to hold its ground than the other errors, and you have touched upon that particular error in your denial of secret sins. You have routed it from its strong-hold and set truth in its place, and when you have gently and tenderly denied the fear and the tumult, and covered yourself or your patient with loving affirmations of trust and comfort, and confidence in the one and only power, you or he will settle down to a state of peace and tranquillity never before experienced.

This disturbance may come after you have denied deceitfulness in its various forms; or perhaps after you have denied sensuality, which will show you that deceit or fleshly appetites was the principal error that caused the physical trouble.

In any case the treatment should be a denial of fear, confusion and whatever symptoms seem most apparent, followed by affirmations of the most tender and comforting expressions of love and trust in the good, as you will feel led to do.

Never look for a patient to chemicalize, lest you bring confusion unnecessarily by your thoughts. The crisis in any case *may* pass without any visible disturbance, and we only explain the condition that you may know how to treat the situation; not to create the anticipation of it

We will further notice the fact that chemicalization never takes place with one who is suffering from erroneous impressions that come from other minds, but is in every instance the result of destroying some stubborn belief or sin in the patient's own character.

It is in this particular that we find the development of the intuition so helpful.

A patient may not be at all aware of the fault that holds him in bondage, while your keen intuitive perception of the situation enables you to relieve him without his finding it out, and his fault or sin will drop out of his life, and perhaps leave him without even a memory of it.

It is in the highest degree important that the practitioner should be firm and fearless in every such emergency.

To become frightened when a patient begins to chemicalize is to lose the advantage you have gained. Treat yourself for courage and trust; and *know* that there is only good.

The student always wants to know how long the patient will be likely to suffer in chemicalization. This depends altogether upon your ability to reach or conquer the stubborn error that holds him.

If he is yielding and receptive you may relieve him with one treatment.

Sometimes it has taken days to conquer the delusion, even when the best of practitioners had the case in hand; sometimes only a few minutes. Each practitioner will find his own way to do in every case.

Every case is a different case, and every difficulty is a result of different causes, or a different combination of causes, but the one eternal **Truth** will heal all, if properly understood.

Each particular symptom of a patient will suggest its own word to the wise practitioner.

If there is fever, your thoughts should be of a cooling, soothing, gentle character; nothing to fear, nothing to fear.

If there are rigors or muscular contractions, give warming, loving thoughts; at the same time be firm and courageous; nothing to fear, nothing to fear.

To any condition that resembles paralysis, or a state of apathy, use sharp, stinging thoughts of an invigorating quality. Such treatment (although silent) will set the life blood bounding with new vigor, and arouse an action perfectly astonishing if one is in perfect accord with true law.

You cover your patient over with your true thoughts, as if bathing him in the fountain of love; you infuse new life into him by your mental presence, and his body responds by unmistakable signs of returning vigor.

All this would be the most absurd nonsense if we were not dealing with mental causes for all physical conditions.

There is no such thing as physical causation.

While we believe in physical causation, the material remedy seems the most rational.

When there is fever in the body, the doctor will always have a plausible theory as to what causes it, and always on a material plane. The nitre cools the fever apparently because of the ages of belief that it possesses that quality, but it never removes the cause.

All causation is in mind; that which produces a seeming evil condition is mortal and false, and stands for rejection. It has no power; is nothing but delusion, therefore we find it wise to hurl the word of truth at it until it crumbles.

The word of truth is the word of the Lord. "The word of the Lord is as a fire, and as a hammer that breaketh the rock in pieces," and "the word of the Lord endureth forever."

ACUTE CASE RELIEVED.

Being called upon (as a last resort) to visit a case of Acute Pleuro Pneumonia, upon which the death sentence had been pronounced *that day* by five physicians, all declaring that nothing could save her; temperature and pulse both up to the highest on record, and every breath a loud gasp very distressing to witness; everything against the case, according to the seeming,—I treated almost continuously from six in the evening till midnight, and next morning at seven o'clock found her breathing quite naturally, with fever nearly gone. Before night she began to throw off the accumulation of mucous, and in three days was out of danger,

She is still well, and knows and acknowledges the truth that saved her to her husband and children. Such acute cases should be treated very much after the manner of treating chemicalization.

LESSON XI.

"Stand fast, therefore, in the liberty wherewith Christ hath made you free, and be not entangled again in the yoke of bondage."

UNTIL you as a student of truth are thoroughly rooted and grounded in the principles of science, and feel a steadfast assurance that it is the open door to all wisdom, you will probably suffer spells of doubt; you will have many misgivings; you will wonder if it is not dangerous to accept what seems to repudiate many of your old settled convictions. Your reason tells you the science is true, and yet you feel afraid.

All this is because you have not fully settled the question as to whether you will serve truth or follow the commandment of man.

If you read the teachings of Christ in the spirit of candor, and study carefully the way He taught, and you desire to follow in that way, you will see how imperative is the need of taking a firm, bold stand on *Principle*, and putting all man-made dogmas under your feet.

If you have really accepted the statements of science, and are at one with them, you will remember that there is but one mind. To rely upon that one mind, which means trusting to Divine wisdom, you will be able to settle all such questions, because Divine wisdom leads you, or prompts you, to let go of all mortality's leadings, and trust Itself wholly.

"Launch out into the deep," if you would secure a goodly draught.

Don't cruise around among the foolish, shallow inconsistencies of mortal mind for truth. You may toil all the days and nights of your life in that way, and nothing but disappointment will come of it.

You have only to remember how little good you have ever realized from such sources; then consider that deep down within every heart there is something that says, "There is good for me." That is the divine prompting to seek in the right direction.

Every real desire of the human heart is for good, and should be satisfied. It *can* be satisfied by going about it according to science, and in no other way.

While believing in the responsibility of mortal mind, you are made aware of its limitation; consequently you believe in ignorance, weakness and unreliability as realities. You don't stop to consider that those words express only negation, that which is not, and you think of ignorance as something real, and perhaps wonder what you shall read to remedy the ignorance.

The books written by people who believe in the reality of ignorance and weakness will not help you out of your darkness at all, because they are in the same error. It would be the blind leading the blind.

You will find their statements as weak and unreliable as your own. We repeat, there is but one mind of which you are a branch. Divine Principle is the vine, and we in our divine nature are the branches, while mortal mind is but the shadow. This one mind is the only Substance in the universe. It is the all Principle, and your reason tells you how to consult it. The apostle James said, "If any man lack Wisdom, let him ask of God."

You ask of God when you consult this Principle, and you get the wisdom by trusting its working Intelligence.

It is the aim of the Science of Mind to educate the conscious mind to *know* what is true. In knowing truth we know God, and when we reason according to this knowledge of God we consult true Principle, which is in reality asking of God.

Now, there is a condition upon which you receive what you ask for, which is that you abide in truth.

Jesus said, "If ye abide in Me, and My words abide in you, ye shall ask what ye will and it shall be done unto you."

To abide in Christ is to abide in Truth, and your receiving what you ask depends upon the accuracy of your reasoning, and your willingness to abide in that line of reasoning, or stand by it, be true to it.

You can readily understand that there must be a great difference between the mind that accepts the whole truth without a doubt of its working power, and the one who doubts and questions every step of the way, and only believes what is proved by sense evidence.

It is the one who awakens the interior perception or intuition who *knows* and understands how Principle works, and whose faith in what it will do is based upon knowledge.

Perfect understanding makes perfect faith, therefore perfect works will follow understanding.

If there is very little understanding there will be very little faith, consequently imperfect demonstrations will be the result.

There may be an intellectual perception of the

philosophy of mental action without fully accepting the teachings as true, but no one can open the mind to a perfect, unbiased understanding of these principles without accepting them. It is impossible.

The very nature of true Principle is to vitalize and awaken a realization of the Divine within us, and when that is accomplished we understand and cannot help accepting.

Whoever talks unbelief in this truth does not understand it, you may be sure, and while you talk unbelief you push away the day of understanding.

It is better to keep silent, even if you think you do not believe, for sooner or later you will have to take back all you say that is not true of Divine Science. After a time you will prove it true in so many ways that you will wonder you ever doubted.

By giving expression to your doubts you dull your comprehension and put off the day of perfect peace.

The same is true in demonstrating over sickness. If you have a case to treat that does not yield, or seems stubborn, it is better never to speak of it unless in a very private way to some one who understands Science, and you want their help on the case. If you are impressed that some error or fault holds a patient in bondage, be careful about giving expression to the thought, and deny the error suggested or named by the impression.

Whoever enters into details by describing a case minutely, with all the bad symptoms as they appear, helps to fix the disease a little closer and make it less yielding.

What we talk about and think much about has a wonderful effect upon our work, and one who persists in talking error or indulges in gossip and calumny cannot hope to succeed.

To be perfectly consistent, we need to completely ignore all evil and all pain; all calumny and discord and evil speaking as well as to cease from thinking evil.

This is the science of silence, and more is accomplished by silent wisdom than by noisy controversy.

Sometimes a case is manifesting health so rapidly under your treatment that you can hardly restrain your delight, and you are tempted to tell a friend how bad the case was when you saw it first, and you relate the whole account, as it seemed to mortal sense, and your friend is amazed at your ability to do as you have with the case, and she relates the whole thing to her friends, and they to their friends, with variations, and the next day you are horrified to find your patient back in the old condition, nearly or quite as bad as ever.

You had forgotten that thinking and wording were building according to your words.

When patients are first healed they are keenly susceptible to every wave of thought, and especially to the thoughts and moods of the one who treats them, and until the health is well established the least said about the case the better, unless every word is in harmony with Divine law.

"A hint to the wise is sufficient." Never talk promiscuously about a case you are treating, and avoid as much as possible having unbelieving minds fixed upon the case while it needs treatment.

A case treated by a student of these lessons just comes to my thought. Being given up to die by physicians and friends, the patient begged for a scientist. Very soon she rallied, and in the course of a few days seemed about to realize perfect health, when she was visited by a relative.

When the relative found her so bright and full of hope and cheer, and learned that it was all attributable to treatments by a Scientist, she began a system of persecution and abuse of the

Science that so shocked the patient in her feeble condition that she died before the next morning.

Had the patient understood the truth for herself, she need not have yielded to the depressing influence of any such foolish persecution, but while dependent upon the understanding of another, and that one absent, she was driven about by popular prejudice, and "the end thereof are the ways of death."

Had the scientist known of the situation at the time, she might have changed the current of the mental influence, but all was over before she knew of it.

Such are the situations we are all called upon to meet, but with steadfast, determined purpose, we shall overcome every obstacle. "The gates of hell shall not prevail against us."

Every seeming obstacle we find in our pathway gives an opportunity to test the law, and every victory over discouragements will lift you to a higher plane spiritually, and increase your understanding and trust of Divine law.

You will rise above the fear that it is presumption to say, "God works through me to will and to do." Every good deed you feel prompted to do, it is God working in you and through you. There is no other Spirit of good to prompt you to good deeds, and whatever you do in spirit and truth, you will be strengthened by that affirmation to yourself, "God works through me to will and to do all that ought to be done by me."

There is great power and strength in the realization that the great Principle of Intelligence, Love and Truth never ceases to work *through* us and *for* us, except when we acknowledge or recognize another power. To keep that realization in mind continually, and let no mortal error come between to darken it, will give you power to heal *instantly*, without argument.

All students of this truth have to begin the work of healing by argument, and by faithful use of the argument as taught in these lessons, your experience will soon teach you to detect the needs of each case you are called upon to treat, and the very word you need to use will often spring spontaneously to your aid.

When you attain to that state of perfect understanding and oneness with Divine Principle, you will be able to heal without argument, and your patients will not be so apt to show chemicalization.

It is the denial of evil passions and old false beliefs that causes chemicalization, but it has to be done. Perfect understanding enables you to speak as Jesus did to the waves, "Peace, be still," and it is done.

Those who have demonstrated that state of perfect oneness with Divine Principle have had to begin at the beginning, just as you are now doing, and they reached that state of oneness with the Father by steadfast loyalty to Principle, and in no other way.

The chemicalization, either in student or patient, is the proof that some stubborn error has not been fully eradicated, and the confusion or disturbance is liable to linger until that error gives place to truth. It has already been disturbed, or it would not strike back, but it has not been dislodged, or it would cease to disturb; therefore the disturbing cause should be routed from its stronghold.

Sometimes a patient is holding malice against some one, and is too proud or too stubborn to yield. In such case, *pride, hatred* and *malice* should be made null and void by denial, followed by the comforting affirmations.

Sometimes deception is the demon that creates the disturbance; if so, treat it the same way. Any fault must be treated the same in tender kindness, but never with censure or blame.

Never indulge in condemnation, no matter how glaring the fault may seem, nor how exasperating.

You can do the case no good so long as you

dwell upon the mortal error as a reality, even in thought; but to contradict its reality effectually causes a vibration which amounts to a tumult till it is quieted by tender words of love.

We will say you have held to that denial, which proved to be the keynote to the trouble, until your patient is quiet, and ceases to complain of unrest or confusion, or ceases to show irritability.

If the disturbance has been severe and prolonged, they now and then complain of great exhaustion after it, as one might who had carried a heavy burden for a long distance, until he trembled and quivered with weariness, and exhaustion compelled him to lay it down. He is relieved of his burden, but still trembles with weakness. So is your patient relieved of his guilty fears.

He is afraid of great prostration, however, and there is fear to conquer as long as any remnant of suffering continues. Exhaustion is sure to suggest death to the patient, if he still believes in death, and there are several false beliefs that are closely related to the belief in death.

A belief in limitation covers the whole ground. It embraces the belief in foolishness, ignorance and weakness, and his great physical exhaustion is the outpicturing of this false belief of the whole human race in limitation, and in foolishness and ignorance.

He forgets that he is a child of dominion; that he is law against all conditions of weather, of climate, of temperature, of diet and of all physical laws.

This law of dominion for the child of God has never made any impression upon *him*, because he believed so thoroughly in limitation, and yet he always admired the dominant qualities in man. A man is not really a man without those dominant qualities.

The signs of the dominant character are Intelligence, Wisdom, Vigor, Vitality, Courage, Endurance, Health, Strength, Boldness and Bravery.

Notice, every one of these dominant characteristics is Godlike in quality, and goes to prove the Divine Sonship of man.

The child of God is not weak, or sick, or foolish, or ignorant, nor lacking in courage and vitality, and to show these negative qualities in any degree is a sign that the ways of mortality have lured him from his Father's house, and made him forget the Omnipotent Source from whence he might gather strength every moment, and the Omniscient Source from which he might gather wisdom at all times, so he trembles with weakness and prostration because of this belief in limitation.

The foolishness and ignorance of the world are holding him in bondage to the mortal belief in death from which *you* are to set him free.

There is no symptom so alarming to you as this terrible prostration, and you need to lean strongly on the Almighty arm, when anybody complains of it. The thought of death is constantly struggling for supremacy in your mind, but you have the all-conquering power of truth on your side, if you stand firm.

You want to deny *fear*, *foolishness* and *ignorance*, and all limitation.

Deny your own belief in limitation. Deny the power of all negation.

Say over and over, There is no death.

After denying all negation thoroughly, begin to affirm, *Love, Love, Divine Love*, and trust and courage and strength. Vigor, vitality, Intelligence, wisdom and *Life, Life, Life*. You are alive with the Life of the Spirit, which is Life everlasting. Eternal Life, perfect Life. You are alive with the Life of the Spirit.

You are strong with the strength of the Spirit.

You are fearless with the courage of Spirit.

Bathe your patient mentally in all the sweet, comforting, soothing, strengthening affirmations that Divine love suggests to you.

To affirm all the dominant qualities in the spirit of love, is the great point for a state of exhaustion.

You are *strong, brave, fearless* and free.

"With long life will I satisfy him, because he hath set his love upon me."

SALT RHEUM CURED.

A lady came for treatment who had been afflicted from childhood with Salt Rheum on the hands and fingers, always being obliged (as she thought) to keep her fingers wrapped in cloths, with salves and liniments; always trying new remedies, and always disappointed in the result.

Never since childhood allowed to do what would necessitate having her hands in water, and always nursing her sore fingers.

She had daily treatments for a week, at the end of which time she was perfectly healed, with hands and fingers as soft and smooth as a child's.

After three years of freedom from the old annoyance she feels secure from any return of it.

LESSON XII.

TOWARD the close of the primary course of lessons, the student of the Science of Mind is very apt to wonder if these principles will work for him as they do for others.

The real inwardness of such mighty principles seems slow in finding its way to the understanding sometimes. There is so much to remember and such a wholesale demolishing of old ideas that have been cherished as true, that much firmness and decision is needed to secure the practical knowledge necessary to turn the Divine Law to account in the solution of the life problem.

The rejection of all evil, and of everything that does not accord with the statement of Divine Being, is the first step to be taken, and every one has to take the first step first. No one can afford to miss this first step, else they will have missed the full cleansing, the seven washings in Jordan.

Even if the seven cleansing denials are all made in one instant, they have to be made; that is, the seven phases of falsity in human belief have got to be erased, whether it is done in five minutes or five years.

The time of its showing forth in perfect freedom depends upon your realization that all those errors are null and void to you.

What are the seven errors so common to mankind that must be erased before perfect peace can be established?

First, The belief in an angry God, and the fear that attends the belief.

Second, The belief in a burning hell, and the fear that attends the belief.

Third, The belief in a personal devil, and the fear that goes with it.

Fourth, The belief in hereditary taint in the flesh, and the fear that goes with it.

Fifth, The belief in sensuality of all kinds, and the fear that goes with it.

Sixth, The belief in deceit, with its fears.

Seventh, The belief in all secret sins that take root in selfishness.

This covers the whole ground.

We will say you understand the basis on which your denial rests, and the process by which you set the Principle into action. You have used your knowledge of this law of mind to erase those false impressions and errors of judgment, and you find yourself free from the bondage to which you were subject while ignorant of your divine right as a child of God.

You are consciously free.

Now, the next step, the next round in the ladder, is to take on; or clothe yourself anew after the cleansing.

This you find is accomplished by affirmations of good, or by the acknowledgment of good as the only reality, and by affirming your rightful inheritance as a child of God, and your dominion over all material environments. This is clothing yourself with conditions in harmony with true law.

You find that by understanding the workings of true law you can trust it; you have faith in what it will do for you, because you know it has its source in Divine Wisdom.

You find that the conscious mind of man may be trained or attuned to perfect harmony with the divine self, thus establishing a consciousness of the oneness of man with the Father.

The branch is one with the vine, but always dependent upon the vine for sustenance and growth.

As the body is always dependent upon the earth for sustenance and supply, so is the mind (which is not a thing of earth at all) dependent upon the great eternal mind for all knowledge, growth and development.

The conscious influx from the Infinite Mind to the human understanding is in proportion to your receptivity. That is, it is not measured bountifully to one and scantily to another, but all have the same source from which to draw and can have all they open the heart to receive.

It comes in the silence.

It is silent communion that inspires the conscious mind to know its relation to the divine self.

It is silent communion that convinces the willing student of the divineness of his birthright.

It is the silent influence we radiate from knowing truth that heals and blesses a friend or patient.

This is called the science of silence; the healing is a silent work. All moral reforms can be accomplished by this silent work, and we may reasonably hope to see the day when people can be taught to know the law by silent communion.

The wonderful power that comes with silent practice (if faithfully pursued) gives a nameless wisdom to know what is wise to say, and when it is wise to say it.

On first learning the power of the word to

change our life conditions, we are very apt to think first of what we can do to set matters all right and make things pleasant for ourselves.

Our greatest concern at first is about our bodily health, then we want our home relations and our family affairs all set in order, which is perfectly right, as harmony at home gives confidence to do for others, and you very soon learn that there is nothing else to be depended on, that Science *has* changing power over all things.

Very soon you begin to think more earnestly of what you can do for others, and what you can do to advance the cause of science and help establish the kingdom of God on earth.

In your progress you discover that the very nature of the law is to make you forget the troublesome self and do for others.

You find it so uplifting to know that the only power in the universe is at your service continually.

You are not afraid when the service of truth takes you through hard passes and dark ways that you would once have thought it impossible to enter, because you realize the constant protection and defense of the Father's love. What once seemed a wearisome task is now a delight. What once seemed to exhaust all physical strength is now made easy.

You find that truly, as you believed, so has it come to pass upon you.

Those who believe in and dread the approach of old age will grow old in appearance.

Those who most effectually erase the human belief in time and declare the belief in old age a fiction, will cease to show the ravages of time or feel the infirmities of old age (so called).

We need not grow old, and to do so is contrary to Godliness; it is mortal delusion, and does not accord with the Christ teaching.

Even on the physical plane it is an absurd delusion, inasmuch as the physical body is constantly renewing itself and is never more than a year old, according to the latest authority on physiology.

Then let us cease to believe the falsehood. As the body is built in accord with the beliefs of the mind, we shall cease to grow old when we cease to believe in old age.

The promise is, "His flesh shall be fresher than a child's; he shall return to the days of his youth."

Every student of Science will prove this statement if he works for it.

To work for it is to put in practice every word of truth that is given you for discipline. You will be all at sea under the various circumstances that surround you and seem so contradictory, unless you *do* put what you know of law into practice.

The *use* of the knowledge you gain enlarges and strengthens the mental forces, the same as the exercise of your physical body promotes health and vigor.

Your thoughts of truth are constantly meeting thoughts of error, and without this knowledge you are at the mercy of all the prevalent false beliefs of the world, which affect you more or less, according to your steadfast reliance upon what you know of truth.

Faithful adherence and fearless declaration of the truth you know is the armor of righteousness, against which the assaults of error are powerless.

Truth is God, therefore Truth is your rock of refuge; Truth is your defense against all error, but it must be recognized and acknowledged in order to have its protecting influence as a safeguard against the appearance we call evil.

The scoffs of unbelievers and the opposition of dogmatism can have no effect to disturb you if you make your knowledge of truth your refuge.

It is only by training the mind to know what is true that you *can* defend yourself against such disheartening influences.

Even reading certain kinds of books will have a depressing effect without the protection of this scientific law. It is very common for invalids to say, it "hurts them to read;" they feel exhausted and depressed after reading ever so little, never dreaming that it is the false quality of the writer's mind that affects them, and they will find that reading from the writings of the one who understands righteous law and lives by Principle will not weary them.

It is not so much the words nor the sentiment but the quality of genuineness that pervades the writings that gives rest and peace.

The spiritually minded soon discover that which brings harmony and peace, and by constant practice they soon learn to detect and put aside the discordant influences.

Steady practice in truth is constant self-defense, and by the steady practice we become a defense and safeguard to all around us. "Neither shall any plague come nigh thy dwelling," is the promise to him that "dwelleth in the secret place of the Most High."

One who thinks only truth and abides in righteous reasoning continually, is the one who dwells in the secret place of the Most High.

The very presence of such is health and peace, and if such wonderful effects are produced without effort, what may we not accomplish by honest, earnest intention to heal and bless?

Our healing thoughts are never lost; they are loving messengers that carry healing to some one, even if they find no entrance into the heart of the one they are intended for.

No true thought, no healing thought, no word of loving intention to heal and bless can possibly be lost; it *must* set the healing forces to work in some mind, somewhere.

The only law under which you rest is that you be faithful in speaking, thinking and radiating truth, health and harmony

The time is now at hand when those who understand may judge of character by the mental atmosphere an individual radiates.

Every one sheds a silent influence corresponding to the character of his thoughts, beliefs and opinions, just as the rose sheds an invisible perfume which all recognize as that of the rose.

And if your thoughts, beliefs and opinions spring from a willing service to truth we shall radiate health and joy, and our very presence will be a benediction.

There is no occasion for a sanctimonious attitude. Sanctimonious piety never gives joy or freedom, but holds one in solemn bondage to form which the heart can never sanction.

So, while devoutly acknowledging God as the only source of health, strength and joy, we claim His bounty as our birthright without debasement or feeling of unworthiness. This true attitude of mind sheds cheerful assurance to others.

We claim all the dominant qualities that are God-like and powerful, because they belong to us as children of God.

They are our inheritance from the Father.

We are children of power, of peace and harmony, and by acknowledging the same with thanks we show forth the power, peace and harmony. God is no respecter of persons. He deals equally with all his children, and if any seem to lack in power or in vigor, health or harmony in *any way*, that one has failed to recognize and claim his own.

The sixth movement of the law, or the sixth treatment of a patient (according to the rule) is the one in which he needs the assurance of his right to claim perfection in every department of his being.

If you are treating yourself, you have already reasoned it out in the study of the lessons, and you make your claim with confidence, because you know upon what it is based; but if you are treating a patient who has not reasoned it out, and is only looking for healing, you have not done for him all you can do, till you assure him of his birthright by silent argument; and you must continue this assurance till he responds by realizing it himself You have already given him the words of courage and trust that relieved him of the fear when he believed that great weakness and prostration were upon him, and he gratefully acknowledges the peace and health your treatments have given him. He says he is perfectly well, and his looks show that he is happy, but he still wants something of you, he does not seem to know just what.

Many practitioners do not recognize this need, but no patient should be discharged without the blessing this need calls for as a sustaining treatment.

You have nothing to deny; you have only to give him a reiteration of the perfection you have already affirmed for him, but the impression must be made deeper, and you will think of many words of courage, strength and enduring trust to add in assuring him of his inheritance, and he should be held in these uplifting thoughts for several days, as security against the mortal error that might otherwise gain the mastery over him again.

Say to him with earnest deliberation and perfect trust in what you say:

You are the perfect creation of the living God. Spiritual like the Father, in harmony with all perfection; fearless and free.

You are perfectly healthy, strong, wise and good.

You have ability and judgment.

You see only good.

You reflect only good.

You reflect the whole universe of goodness in health, strength, vigor, vitality, courage and endurance.

You are perfect because you are a child of perfection.

You are wise because you are a child of wisdom, and you reflect wisdom from every quarter.

Ability, judgment, health, strength and peace are your rightful inheritance, and no one can deprive you of them.

Your peace flows like a river.

From every source and through every avenue comes goodness and perfection to bless and strengthen you.

You are compassed about with truth, goodness and strength, through which no evil can reach you.

The Divine Life is lived within you perfect. In the Divine Life is vigor, vitality, health, strength, peace and joy for evermore.

You know it, and realize it.

You acknowledge it with gratitude.

You are happy, fearless and free.

You are perfectly well and sound and strong, mentally, morally and physically.

You abide in the truth that makes free.

The Lord will bless you, and keep you, and cause his face to shine upon you for evermore.

These are true thoughts that may be given to any one under any circumstances, because they are the truth regarding the child of God.

In these words you speak of spiritual perfection without reference to what appears in the flesh at all.

This is sowing to the Spirit.

"For he that soweth to his flesh shall of the flesh reap corruption; but he that soweth to the Spirit shall of the Spirit reap life everlasting."

It is clearly sowing to the flesh when we think and calculate for the flesh as the real man; and we know and prove that thinking and realizing only Spiritual perfection, makes the man of flesh manifest that perfection.

Never doubt your own ability to demonstrate over every seeming difficulty.

Doubt is the demon that deprives you of success in your attempts to demonstrate truth. You must know that there is no situation, circumstance or condition in life that you may not master if you *will*.

Cold and heat, fire and frost, storm and tempest, wind and flood are your servants, not your masters.

We may truly say, I love the cold and the heat; I love the storm and the tempest; I love the wind and the flood; I love all that has been called dangerous for mankind, because I glorify God in proving it powerless to harm me.

God is glorified in every instance where His children overcome error and the fear of evil happenings.

If you think you have an enemy, say to him (mentally), There is only love between us. You are a child of Divine Love. You *are* love.

Persist in these affirmations patiently, and pay no attention to what seems to contradict them, and you will turn his enmity to love. To recognize enmity is to foster and nourish it.

The same is true of sickness and pain.

You defile the temple of God when you say, I am sick, I am weak, I am in pain, or I am unworthy.

"Know ye not that ye are the temple of God, and that the Spirit of God dwelleth in you? If any man defile the temple of God, him shall God destroy; for the temple of God is holy, which temple ye are."

The moment you admit sickness, pain or disease you withdraw your conscious support of the Spirit in the measure of your complaint. The likeness and image of your error is made manifest in an increase of discord, disease and discomfort.

Never place the false word, the negative after the "I am," not even in thought, for the word or thought has power to bring forth. The false shows forth in *seeming* only, according to mortal belief. The *true* shows forth in *reality*, according to Divine Law.

"By thy words thou art justified," means by the word of truth is justification manifest.

"By thy words thou art condemned," means that all condemnation is begotten of false words.

A man's word is his only burden, said the prophet, therefore it is wisdom to speak only of Divine perfection.

Let the positive good follow the "I am" always. I am well; I am strong; I am wise; I am free; I am able; I am perfect, because I am the child of Perfection.

I am compassed about by the law of perfection and goodness, and no evil can touch me, for in the realm of reality there is only good.

"May the Lord bless thee, and keep thee, and cause his face to shine upon thee," and may thy heart open to receive the truth that will prove thy shield and buckler.

BLINDNESS CURED.

An elderly gentleman who was totaly blind from cataract, and suffering intense agonies from neuralgia, embracing all of one side of the head, the eye swollen and protruding, had not slept an hour at a time for over a year in consequence of the pain, came to the city to consult physicians, who had decided to remove the right eye and operate upon the other. As he was about to be taken to the hospital a kind friend, who had been healed by Divine Science, came in and persuaded him to try it.

He was treated and went away relieved of all pain; slept soundly all night, which he had not done before for a year. He came for treatment the two succeeding days, after which he returned to his home in the country and was treated absently.

In about three weeks he wrote that he could see to read the papers with his best eye, and with the other he could count his fingers by holding them up to the light. Absent treatments were continued for about three months, after which we received word that he was perfectly healed, and he praised God for his delivery from the hands of the surgeon, and for his rescue from a world of darkness.

CONCLUSION.

AFTER perusing these lessons for the first time, the student is very apt to falter and hesitate about accepting all the statements.

This is because he has not yet reasoned it out from the basic principles, and the only remedy is to go over the whole ground deliberately, (again and again if necessary) till every statement is clearly understood.

The benefits of science, the peace, comfort and assurance that science is true, will not be fully realized while one fears to depart from the old ways that darken his life.

Do you feel that you do not understand?

Then say to yourself *mentally*, "Nothing can stand between me and the knowledge of truth thut will liberate me from all error.

Meditate upon this declaration, *hold to it*, and reason it out on the basis of the absolute allness of the Good, the Omnipresent Wisdom, and Omnipotent Power.

Then affirm, "I *can* know. I *can* understand."

Then I *do* know. I *do* understand.

Affirm that you *can*, till it becomes a fixed conviction of the mind, and in the regular sequential order of unfoldment you will find it easy to say, I *do*.

To begin without any scruples about it, and say, I *do* understand. I *do* know. I *am* able, etc., is still better; but to those who think they *dare* not we should advise the more gradual proceeding.

When you realize the full meaning of the "*I am*," you will not be afraid to say I *do* understand. I *do* know.

You will rather be afraid to say, I can't, or I don't know.

Never put the negative word after the "I am" in any case.

I can't. I don't know, and I'm afraid, belong to the old dispensation of darkness and negation. The "I am" is in the present, the positive declaration of what is *now*.

So fear not to say, I *can* understand *now*. I do understand *now*. I have Divine Wisdom *now*. I am the perfect child of God *now*.

Hold to this persistently, and "thy light shall break forth as the morning, and thy health shall spring forth speedily."

Throw all doubt and fear to the winds, and declare, I am under the protection of Almighty Goodness, Wisdom and Love, and nothing but good can reach me.

When days of darkness and discouragement seem to overcome, these are the words that will restore peace and harmony, if used with trust.

If beset with opposition and persecution according to the ways of mortal mind, say to yourself, there is no power but of God, and I am free from all evil, and from all discord that comes of mortal error. God is my refuge; in Him I trust. I am fearless and free.

If you still believe in and fear headaches, or indigestion, or the danger of taking cold, say, NO. There is no life or sensation in matter, and I have dominion over my flesh; I am Spirit and I cannot take cold or suffer a headache or indigestion. Only the good is true.

As the will of God is only good, and my human will is merged in the Divine will, I am one with Divine perfection, and I will show forth that perfection in my flesh.

I am perfectly well and sound and strong in every part.

I am free from even the belief in headaches, indigestion, or taking cold. Hold to such thoughts till you realize freedom.

If you still feel wearied with your daily cares, and your duties seem burdensome, take a few moments to yourself in the silence, and meditate upon the absolute perfection of Spirit, and the impossibility of Spirit being weary. Say, God is my rest, God is my peace, and I have strength and endurance unlimited. I am at rest.

Such thoughts held for a few moments will remove all weariness, and you soon *know* that true thinking is the only sure panacea for every ill.

If you think you are wronged or injured in any way, mentally deny that anything or anybody in in the whole world can injure you by word or deed.

To any individual that you think is inclined to wrong you, call the name mentally and say your intentions toward me are *only good*, and everything you say and do is a help and advantage to me and also to yourself. There is only love between us, and only love in your heart.

No matter how contrary things may seem, hold to this line of thought and the good will conquer. Many ask if it is right to treat for temporal blessings such as money and other material needs.

It is certainly right to trust God for whatever we seem to lack that is good, the same as to pray for the temporal blessing of health. As it is good to have abundance and be free from harassing care, it is right to treat for just what you need.

All good is the gift of God; so it is the good law or law of God that provides the abundance.

When poverty stares you in the face (according to the seeming) you may know that the adversity is the result of adverse calculations in your problem.

The adversary in this case is your dependence upon what mortal mind says, without reference to Divine Principle.

You set the law into action in a manner adverse to righteousness, and the consequence is adversity in temporal affairs.

How have you made the law work adversely?

By a belief in limitation which caused fear and doubt regarding the outcome of your plans. The fear and doubt brought forth what you expected; then the complaining and bemoaning your ill success increased the difficulty, and you held still more strongly to the belief that you were unfortunate.

The fear, the complaints and admissions of "bad luck" (so called) sets the law to work in appearance on the adverse or negative side.

You acknowledge a false power every time you complain of adversity.

You recognize a phantom as reality every time

you admit poverty; you *name* it as something *not good*, and it stays by you as long as you admit it.

It is all a mistake. Not a word of it is true.

The remedy is to reason yourself out of the belief by denying the poverty and everything that tends to limitation.

Deny adversity and the fear of it. Deny that one can have more than another, or better judgment or more ability than another.

In short, set your conscious mind into harmoney with Divine Goodness and love, which means abundance of all that is good.

Your denials will remove every obstacle to perfect realization, which comes by affirming the abundance you desire as already received.

Hold to your affirmations with trust, and praise and thank God for abundance, even if you haven't a penny. Give praise and thanks to the Giver of all good, and keep affirming abundance as already yours. Be patient and true to the Principle, and abundance will come to you, sometimes in very unexpected ways.

You set the law to work in righteousness by praise and thanksgiving; while by the adverse plan you unconsciously push away the very thing you want by complaining and by admitting the *not good,*

Never tell anybody you are poor, no matter how apparent the poverty is to mortal sense; the abundance will never come by naming the lack of abundance. You invoke the negative forces (or what seems a force) when you name it or give it a conscious recognition in mind as a reality.

You also invoke the Almighty Principle of goodness. Jehovah Jireh, the Provider, when you acknowledge it as all, and praise and glorify it as your only refuge, defense and supply.

Your acknowledgment and trust of this great providing power sets the law into action, just as surely as the touch of the harp strings sets them to vibrating.

If the touch is made by the trained and skilled musician, the vibration will be harmonious and sweet; but if made by the awkward, untaught hand it will be discordant.

So it is with all who use these mighty principles for the harmonizing of life's conditions.

The mind must be trained to know the laws of harmony in mental action, and thus be able to bring harmony out of discord in every department of our being.

The same principles may be applied to every problem that has a righteous end in view, by first rooting out every plant that our heavenly Father

(Divine Principle) hath not planted. and planting the true word in its place.

The kingdom of heaven is the kingdom of harmony, and it "cometh not by observation," but by knowing the true way and walking in it, and "It is the Father's good pleasure to give you the kingdom."

THE END.

INDEX.

	PAGE
LESSON I.	
God the only power,	13
Cure of consumption by the lessons,	43
LESSON II.	
Freedom by denial,	45
Statement of Being,	57
Paralysis healed by lessons alone,	84
LESSON III.	
The power of the Word in affirmation,	85
Self-discipline,	111
Eczema cured by lessons and treatments,	113
LESSON IV.	
The work of the mind,	114
Asthma cured by lessons and treatments,	139
LESSON V.	
Confidence or faith in the Word,	140
Dyspepsia cured by lessons alone,	170
LESSON VI.	
Get understanding,	171
Rheumatism cured,	194
TESTIMONIALS,	195, 196, 197, 198

INDEX.

Part Second.

PAGE.

Lesson VII.
The Word that heals, ... 199
A case of aneurism cured, . . . 218

Lesson VIII.
Deceitful influences, ... 219
Bright's disease cured, ... 236

Lesson IX.
Forgiveness of sin, ... 238
Cancer healed, ... 253

Lesson X.
Divine love versus mortal fear, . . 255
Acute case of pleuro pneumonia healed, 277

Lesson XI.
Freedom made manifest, . . . 279
Salt rheum cured, ... 292

Lesson XII.
Completeness acknowledged, . . 293
Blindness by cataract cured, . . 308

Conclusion, ... 309